T0158970

From the Heart of a Child

of a Child

Our Incredible Journey

Florence B. Kinney

Inspiring Voices®

A Service of **Guideposts**

Inspiring Voices books may be ordered through booksellers or by contacting:

Inspiring Voices
1663 Liberty Drive
Bloomington, IN 47403
www.inspiringvoices.com
1-(866) 697-5313

Because of the dynamic nature of the Internet, any web addresses or links contained in this book may have changed since publication and may no longer be valid. The views expressed in this work are solely those of the author and do not necessarily reflect the views of the publisher, and the publisher hereby disclaims any responsibility for them.

Any people depicted in stock imagery provided by Thinkstock are models, and such images are being used for illustrative purposes only.

ISBN: 978-1-4624-0299-1 (sc)
ISBN: 978-1-4624-0300-4 (e)

Library of Congress Control Number: 2012916161

Certain stock imagery © Thinkstock.

Printed in the United States of America

Inspiring Voices rev. date: 9/18/2012

Contents

Dedication

I dedicate this book to
the Glory of God

The Father, Son & Holy Spirit
Whose word has been a lamp to guide
our feet and a light for our path.

*This book is written
in loving memory of
my husband, Charles.*

List of Illustrations

Acknowledgments

With deepest humility and love, I give thanks to my Heavenly Father, His Son, Jesus Christ, and the precious Holy Spirit for the "calling" of our ministry. I am grateful for the moment heaven and earth met, when our lives were transformed by a Divine Being, who has been faithful to walk with us through the joys and the tears of an incredible journey. His lamp always enlightening our minds; His light illuminating our pathways.

I gratefully acknowledge my dear friends and sisters-in-Christ, Diane Maier, Pastor Karen Gibson and Gail Fannis for their encouragement and vision that made this book of inspiration possible. You had a vision for this writing and were determined to see that vision come into being.

To Diane, there are not enough words for me to express my gratitude for all the ways in which you have touched my life with your faith and inspiration. Your wonderful works of art in typing and shaping this manuscript has brought joy to my soul. The long hours you have devoted to this work, speak of the passion you hold within your heart for sharing the Word and love of God with others. I will forever be grateful to you for the sharing of your vision, time and talents. I could not have completed this book without your belief in and support of this ministry. Thank you, dear friend.

To Pastor Karen, prayer warrior, thank you from the bottom of my heart for the beautiful uplifting prayers you have offered up to heaven on my behalf and for this ministry. You have always been there encouraging and sharing your vision with me. You have brought me closer to the angels and their comforting presence in my life. I love residing at Angels Crossing, where lives are touched, changed and miracles happen. Thank you, dear friend.

To Gail, your encouragement and support of this ministry has meant so much to me. Your vision for this book has been most inspirational. Thank you for searching out the wonderful front cover image. I know you spent much time scrolling through many images, searching for just the right one. The image of a seeking child praying amid the light of hope for a better tomorrow, I pray will be an inspiration to thousands. I am also grateful to have you as my "ministering partner" bringing God's love and light to others. Thank you, dear friend.

My deepest gratitude to my family, both near and far, who believed in the calling Charles and I received. Your response of encouragement, time, and gifts of support have made a difference in the lives of less fortunate children. To my great-nephew, Hunter Davis, thank you for the wonderful sketches found in this book. Thank you, Hunter, for sharing your beautiful artistic talent with others. I am so proud and pleased you are a part of the Lord's story.

To my niece and God-daughter, Laura Ball, for your lovely words of inspiration, I will always cherish. I shall never forget the young lady who drove one hundred miles round trip so I could purchase special rag dolls for the children. You performed this act of love so willingly and cheerfully, and it meant the world to me. I shall always remember our special time together. I hope you will also.

Now to our family of "elves" and to the community at large, a simple thank you seems much too small. We could not have reached out to thousands of children, both hurting and in need, without you! Each of you have made a huge difference in the lives of many. We shall be forever grateful.

I pray God will bless each of us with His love and light, drawing us ever closer to Him. I pray "His story" in this book will inspire thousands around the world to respond with love toward one another. It is my prayer and desire of my heart, you will reach out to the hurting, needy and the lost, touching them with your "gift of hope." From the heart of a child, I wish you a most incredible journey.

Foreword

"Meema, did you ever count how many times your life was changed in 15 minutes? Mine was going into Mrs. Kinney's house tonight and meeting her. I'll never be the same." These are words spoken by a ten year old child to his grandmother after a visit to Santa's Workshop. From the mouths of babes—this is exactly how I felt the first time I crossed the threshold into Santa's Workshop a.k.a. Angels Crossing.

For years I had contributed toys and games for Charles and Florence Kinney's project, Santa's Workshop for Hospitalized Children, dropping them in a collection box in the vestibule of our church. My young sons would always pick something out when we were Christmas shopping. It wasn't until I actually got involved at the Workshop that I began to understand the scope of the project. It is truly amazing.

As you turn the pages of this book you will see how their incredible journey unfolds. I can only think of the proverbial pebble dropped in the water sending out ripples that have no conceivable end. From two toy trucks to 54,000 gifts of love and hope. You will learn how Florence and Charles received their "calling" for this ministry and how they extended an invitation for family, friends, and the community to help. People have been and still are drawn to participate in this ministry in some very miraculous ways.

Florence has had this story in her heart for a couple of years now. The time is right! The words just flowed like a river and in four months time she had a book. I'm glad that this "little ol' country girl" decided to share God's story through her story from the heart of a child.

It is my prayer that this book stirs you, the reader, to listen to and see God at work in your life. What ministry might He be calling you to?

Diane Maier
Lay Leader, Union Hill UMC

Introduction

We were created to serve an awesome God ~ a God who reaches down through time and space and touches the heart of His child in immeasurable ways. It has been my privilege and honor for the past twenty-two years to serve an awesome God in an awesome way, watching Him at work in the lives of little children, caught up in the adversities of life through illness and need.

In the following pages, you will read how God can send His love and comfort through a stuffed animal, a book, a dolly and yes, even a toy truck.

Is it possible to make a difference in a child's life by such means? The answer is a resonating Yes! Do we have a God who sends miracles to make it all possible? Yes, we do! We have a God who has a "storehouse of supply" which knows no end. Whether it be a child in recovery, a child about to enter Eternity, or simply a child in material need, God is there!

You may wonder where are we in all of this? Where do we fit into the picture? In the following pages, I hope to share with you our incredible journey into the hearts of ill and needy children. Children, who not only feel the pain of body, but the pain within their heart; the hope of belonging, of being loved, of knowing someone cares even if it is a stranger.

It is frightening for little children being hospitalized and find themselves in strange surroundings. It is even more frightening and sad when it is Christmas. The togetherness of family, the decorated tree and the special hope of a dream being realized is lost and loneliness enters their heart until they experience the love of God through strangers.

Today, nearly 54,000 hurting children and their families have known "the touch of God's love" through a God-called ministry and it all began with two little toy trucks.

May God's love warm your heart as you journey with me through the following pages, as we all are His children and we all need to be loved. Yes, it has truly been an incredible journey!

Florence B. Kinney

Chapter 1

In The Beginning

*"Being confident of this very thing, that He who hath begun a good work in you will perform it until the day of Jesus Christ." **Philippians 1:6***

It was September 1989. Fall was on the horizon and the leaves of autumn had begun changing color. For my husband, Charles, and I, it would not only be a change of season, but also a change of dwelling as well. We had just sold our home and were moving to our new home in a neighboring county. This home that was awaiting us had an urgency about it that we could feel, but not understand. We had viewed several other homes, but after viewing this particular home, I had dreams of it for three consecutive nights. There appeared to be a "knowing" within me, this particular home would be ours.

I shared this feeling with my husband at the time. We put in an offer and the realtor said it would never be accepted. It was much too low. I told him it was all we could afford and I felt it would be accepted, because I felt we were supposed to buy that particular home.

Back then, there was so much happening that we did not understand. Today, as I reflect back, I understand fully. Our offer was presented that evening. At 11:00 p.m. we received the call telling us our offer had been accepted. There was not even a counter offer made and the realtor was amazed! The "knowing" I felt within me certainly came true. What seemed even more fascinating was how quickly the home was placed in our name. There was an urgency in the air, so to speak, that was very prevalent. Now tiers and tiers of filled cartons, displaced furniture, papers to sign and last minute errands to run filled our agenda. Soon the sounds of the moving van came closer and our journey to our new home had begun.

Getting settled seemed overwhelming as we both had to report to our jobs every day and try to get our home in order in the meantime. After several weeks, we finally were back to routine. However, just a few weeks before Christmas, that routine would be altered by a newspaper clipping.

Our city newspaper was printing human interest stories for the holidays. One of these stories drew my attention. It told of two little brothers who would be spending Christmas in the hospital as they would be undergoing surgery.

The article stated how disturbing hospitalization can be for little children, finding themselves away from home and in strange surroundings, no matter what time of year, but even sadder and lonelier at the holidays. Christmas time was especially difficult for little ones to handle. As I read the article, I was deeply moved, but then daily routine beckoned me. For the next few days my thoughts kept returning to that article.

Finally, one evening I had a conversation with Charles and related my feelings of sadness and concern for these little brothers. I suggested maybe we could cheer them up a bit if we took them each a little toy truck.

"What do you think?" I asked.

He smiled answering in the affirmative. We purchased two little toy trucks, wrapped them in children's Christmas paper, put their names on tags signed from "Santa". We delivered them to the local hospital. They were given anonymously at the information desk, and we quickly left. For us, it was just an act of kindness and it warmed our hearts.

A few days passed and there began a stirring within me, thoughts of other ill children who would not be home for Christmas. Could we make a difference in their Christmas? I pondered all these thoughts until my heart was bursting for action. I knew I had to tell my husband what was going on in my head. Nervously I asked him if we could bring a smile and a surprise to a few more children. With a puzzled look on his face, he said, "Well, I guess so, but this is it now. We aren't rich Hon (name he always called me) and we have our own responsibilities." I so remember that conversation and I agreed it would be the last time I would ask. I called the hospital, told them of our plan and would it be agreeable on their end. They were thrilled and excited! They advised us what a difference that would make in the children's holiday stay. We advised the administrator they would be gifts from "Santa" and the children and their families were not to know who gave them.

So off to the store we went. Overflowing basket carts of toys, dollies, games, books, followed along with reams upon reams of children's wrapping paper, bows and whatever else was needed. Upon our arrival home, we counted four hundred gifts. We were shocked to say the least, but what a fun time! It seemed like we had just relived a part of childhood. It felt like we too, were kids again.

We delivered the car load of gifts, once again anonymously, with brightly colored paper, bowed with love, labels stating age levels, boy or girl, and tags reading "from Santa".

And so the fall of moving turned into the winter of giving and sharing and loving a stranger's child. Little did we know that there was another hand in all of it. A hand we did not see at that time. Never could we have dreamed that someone in another realm of existence was watching and planning our future, His hand extended toward a man and a woman with a heart for HIM and His little children.

Chapter 2

The Calling

"Suffer little children to come unto me, and forbid them not: for of such is the kingdom of God." **Luke 18:16**

The fall of 1990 arrived in all its glory. Cool breezes and "colorful dressed" trees dotted the landscape. The routine of days filled our agenda until one evening when we received a phone call from the hospital where we had delivered four hundred Christmas gifts the year before. The lady asked if we would be giving gifts again this year for the children in their pediatric ward. I advised her we would not be doing anymore. I explained it had been a one-time gesture only, but we appreciated her call. Hearing the disappointment in her voice was sad, but I remembered the promise I made to my husband. I promised him it would be a one-time effort.

Shortly thereafter upon returning from work one evening, we received another phone call. This time it was from another local hospital, well known for working with cancer children. The head administrator from Child Life was on the phone. She advised me that she had been at a joint hospital administrative meeting and heard about our giving to the other hospital. She wondered if we would consider their pediatric unit for Christmas.

She thought it was a wonderful endeavor and it would mean so much to the children there at the holidays. I advised her, with much sadness, that we would not be doing it again as we could not afford to purchase gifts for so many youngsters. She understood, but again, I would hear the disappointment in her voice.

A few nights later, a third local hospital called. This person calling had also "heard the news" at the joint administrative meeting. She asked if their hospital could also be "on our list." Once again, I declined and by now I was saddened along with everyone else. At that point in time we had no idea our lives were about to change forever. That same week we received a call from a reporter at our city newspaper. He was doing "human interest" stories for the holidays and learned of our giving to the original hospital through hospital news reported events. This gentleman asked if he could come to our home and do an interview with us. I told him we would not be doing anything this time around so an interview would not be warranted. He said he was sorry to hear that, as it was difficult for ill children to be away from home at the holidays, especially in strange and scary surroundings. He had been advised what joy the children had experienced the year earlier.

By now Charles and I were perplexed by all the phone calls. Then, again, a repeated call – the one that would make a difference. It was from the same reporter at the newspaper. He said, "I don't mean to bother you, but I have a question for you. Have you prayed about your decision?"

I was taken aback by his question, as I remember a moment of silence between us. Then shyly I answered, "No."

He said, "Mrs. Kinney, I wish you would. You just might change your mind."

When my husband, Charles, returned from work that evening, I told him immediately about the call. I told him we needed to pray as I felt something was happening. We prayed, asking for guidance and direction for our lives and for God's will to be fulfilled. At that **very moment**, we received a warmth that trickled through our entire beings and a joy so deep, we knew those calls had originated from Heaven. With tears streaming down our faces, we had no doubt at all. We had received a wonderful calling!

God had used messengers in order to get our attention–hospital personnel, administrators, and especially a newspaper reporter. Little did we know then how great and miraculous this calling would be. We learned quickly there is nothing on earth more wonderful and exciting than to be called to work "in the Lord's vineyard". It would turn out to be a privilege and honor to serve Him and His little children.

We notified the hospitals that, YES, we would be bringing gifts to them and they were overjoyed to hear the news.

Now our question was how are we going to do it? We were talking about taking Christmas to several hundred children and we were folks who lived week to week on our paychecks. We were not rich financially, so this would be a challenge. What we had not learned at this juncture was that we would need to depend upon a higher power in another realm. It would be absolutely imperative that our Lord be the center of this endeavor and we knew He would then handle all our concerns and would guide our pathways.

And then, one more call would be received. One more request to add to "our list". This time a mental health center for disturbed and abused children–children removed from their homes, who felt the world was against them. Would we add them to "our list"?

Yes, indeed, for the Lord would provide. They belonged to Him and needed to feel loved. Our calling had been received. Now, what was the next step?

At this particular time, my husband worked part time at a local grocery store. He mentioned our new endeavor to a few co-workers and shortly thereafter we were invited to place tags on their community Christmas tree which was intended to bring holiday joy to a needy child. This same invitation was extended to other groups and organizations in the community.

We put family and friends to work cutting out Christmas tags in the form of angels. These were cut from the fronts of Christmas cards and we would list toy suggestions given to us by the hospitals on the back of these tags, ribbon them and place them on the store's community tree. We would pray the community would respond. We placed only one hundred tags on this tree, so there would be plenty of room for other charitable causes. This meant several hundred gifts would need to be purchased. So we began asking our family and close friends to join us in bringing a smile to an ill and needy child.

At the store the community response was wonderful. Gaily wrapped packages began to arrive and we were on our way. My husband and I found ourselves back in store toy aisles filling up store carts, one after another. With family and friends helping us, eight hundred wonderful gifts were distributed anonymously. That was double the amount from the year earlier. We were on our way to an incredible journey. All we lacked now was a name for our project. Again, prayer was involved.

"Santa's Workshop for Hospitalized Children" was born–a name that would become well known by many in our community over the course of the next twenty-two years.

Now I realized why I had three dreams in the fall of 1989 concerning our new home. This home contained a huge family room where a number of folks could sort, process, wrap and bow hundreds of gifts. There were also more rooms in our current home–rooms that would be needed for processing and storing of gifts.

Our former home was small and would not have the storage area we would need as the project grew. God knew even then what we would need. God is so good all the time!

Chapter 3

The Gathering

"For where two or three are gathered together in my name, I am there in the midst of them." **Matthew 18:20**

In the fall of 1991 requests and suggestions for gifts began arriving in early October. This was a good thing, as it gave us more time for shopping and processing. However, the number of requests began increasing and it became evident we would need help. It was time Mr. & Mrs. Claus had some "elves" at Santa's Workshop.

I was an Avon representative at the time, having sold for thirty-five years, and my thought was to share our need with some of my customers. I shared with those who had become close friends as well as loyal purchasers. Nine responded positively and said they would be glad to help sort, wrap, label and whatever else was needed. My Mom was an elf from the very beginning in both purchasing and processing gifts. Over the years she would wrap thousands of activity sets and took charge of the nursery and baby gifts.

We now had ten "elves", and with Mr. & Mrs. Claus we made a gathering of twelve. As I reflect back, it was the same number of disciples our Lord gathered for his ministry on earth.

As the weeks passed we knew we would need more revenue to purchase hundreds of gifts. Therefore, we needed to put a plan into action. We decided to purchase candy bars at wholesale and sell them to businesses in the community. A list of businesses was drawn up and we began contacting each one. A number of them responded in the affirmative and our little candy business was born. This was the first step to involve community on this type of level. We only made cents on the dollar, but at least it was something.

Each day we would gather for lunch around the dining room table, join hands and pray for each child recipient and their families. We knew in our heart that a spiritual power was present–not only because of His promise, but because this was HIS PROJECT and not ours. We knew if we kept Him at the very center of His project, He would direct our pathways in ways known only to Him.

At this point in time, the mental health center for problematic children sent us their wish list, which they have done for many years. Their list covered such items as board games (#1 on the list), books, toys, stuffed animals, craft sets and even footballs and basketballs. The board games were used for interaction purposes, enabling the children to create friendships with one another, since little cottages were now their home away from home.

Their suggestions began with infant and ended with teenagers fourteen to eighteen years of age.

Should you wonder about the infant part, I will explain it. Many babies in the area were born with health problems due to bad vices and the hospitals would send them to the mental health center on a temporary basis, always with the hope of rejoining baby and parent at a later time. Therefore, there were many baby needs such as blankets, bedding, rattles, and personal care items. Santa's Workshop was a proud sponsor of those items as well. This wish list proved to be a wonderful way for us to shop, knowing that what we purchased was truly needed.

Soon a suggestion list arrived from one of the hospitals along with a paper of toy safety guidelines. Fire regulations forbid electrical or friction producing toys. Toys had to be sturdy with no sharp edges and non-toxic. Also all toys had to be new. Medical games and toys were not appropriate, as the hospitalized child was already fearful.

Because of the diversity of religious beliefs, a religious item would not be accepted. This fact saddened us, but it was imperative we adhere to the rules and respect everyone's faith. Remembering that all gifts were wrapped upon delivery, hospital personnel put great faith and trust in our work. Not one item would leave our home until I had approved its release. We never had a complaint of any kind and all rules were followed explicitly, as they are to this very day.

As more and more requests came in, we realized that a system needed to be put into place, where everything would move along in an orderly fashion. The project was broken down into three different segments. The first segment would be the three hundred activity sets, which needed to be sorted down as sets and then wrapped. These sets are gauged for the three to five and six to eight age level. A set consisted of a jumbo coloring book, a ten to twelve piece tray puzzle, a story book, a fun activity pad and a box of 24 count Crayola crayons. The hospitals were overjoyed to receive them and they are still the number one request today.

The second segment would be dollies and stuffed animals. Even there we had to be careful no stuffed animal had shaggy long hair. This type of hair was a problem for asthmatic children and those with other respiratory problems. Only short haired or velveteen animals were selected.

The third segment would be games and toys. The hospitals preferred all USA games and toys that followed their safety guidelines.

We had called our "elves" aboard and we had a workable system in place so we now were on our way to brightening hundreds more children's lives.

Up to this point we had mainly given gifts to pediatric in ward patients in the hospitals and filled their play rooms with new toys for the upcoming year. This time we would learn that gifts were being distributed in additional areas such as emergency, social work, nursery, rehabilitation, mental health units and outpatient. We were asked if a child was released a day or two before Christmas, could they also receive a Santa gift. We said it would be our pleasure to do so. That way, no child would be left out. Everyone would experience God's love and our love through their gift. They would not be forgotten; instead they would feel loved.

You may wonder where was God in all of this? He was front and center, just as He is today, touching the lives of ill and needy children, doctors, nurses, elves and families. The joy of having elves singing Christmas carols while working was music to my ears. Laughter rang out in room after room and everyone loved what they were doing. What beautiful memories would be ours to cherish.

As the holiday approached we would deliver twelve hundred brightly wrapped gifts to four different locations. One hundred gifts came in from angel tags hung on the Community Christmas Tree. The other eleven hundred were purchased by family, elves and Mr. & Mrs. Claus.

What a "holy experience" to bring a "moment of joy" to hundreds of God's children; yet never fully realizing what lay before us. Hundreds of gifts would turn into thousands of gifts, all under the watchful eye of the Master. It would all be part of our incredible journey.

From the Heart of a Child

If I could, I would hug you just

like I do my teddy bear

I would place a kiss upon your

cheek, if I could be there.

I would snuggle up on your knee;

hope a story might be told

My little friend might fall asleep;

she is yet to be one year old.

If I could, I would reach up and

gently squeeze your hand

Through misty eyes, I'd try to say

I think you're mighty grand.

You know, for just a little while,

my illness held no dread

As Santa gleefully made a "special

visit" right there at my bed.

My hospitalized Christmas Day
was truly made complete
With books, puzzles, games and
toys; even slippers for my feet.
I know this made my Mom and Dad
more cheerful on this day
As they hope I now will return to
normal health and play.

So thank you everyone for sharing and for caring
For the dollies and the teddies Santa came bearing.
In remembering us, you gladdened
the heart of a little child
And that's what Christmas is about:
a little one meek and mild.

Florence B. Kinney

Chapter 4

The Greatest of These is Love

*"And now abide faith, hope, love, these three, but the greatest of these is love." **I Corinthians 13:13***

God is love! Where there is love, God is. Where God is, there is love. One of the most asked questions we heard over the years, was "Why do you do this? Why do you put yourselves through all this work and financial giving when you do not know the children or their families?"

I have only two answers to give. First, when you are called by God to do His will for your life and for the lives of others, you respond out of love for the Master, the one who loved us before we ever knew how to love. Secondly, you respond out of love for one another, and for us, our focus was to be on His little children who were hurting and needed compassion and love. For me, I could not have loved my own child any greater than I have loved a stranger's child. I believe God gave my husband and me "the heart of a child" so we could feel their pain and relate to their suffering. To see the suffering with one's own eyes changes everything. A baby fighting for life in an oxygen tent, a little soul with no hair, a child who has been so abused he no longer speaks. Children called "the forgotten ones", who only see doctors and nurses, and never a loved one, all are part of the answer to the question "Why?" This is all part of the world we live in, and the greatest gift we can offer is our love.

During the year of 1992 we realized we would need to plan and shop throughout the year in order to meet the needs that had arisen that year. We were moving from a few hundred children with needs to beyond a thousand youngsters. In this particular year more and more families were losing jobs, were encumbered with debt from medical bills and we were being told many children would not be having any Christmas. We knew this could not happen under God's watch, so we took on additional areas within the hospital unit where needs were great. Our little project was growing quickly. We now found ourselves supplying eighty-five rattles to new born babies, taking gifts to children with family crises, children with autism, attention deficit, and other children emotionally and mentally challenged. It no longer was just a child lying in a hospital bed. We were being spread out in all directions.

We had now received the first suggestion about needed clothing. We added that to our agenda, and we were able to send the first four cartons of new clothing out that year.

In order to continue spreading out into different areas we knew we would have to have more community taking part, so we decided to purchase small Christmas trees, decorate them with angel tags and take them to local businesses, just as we were doing with candy bars. We went from business to business asking if they would accept a small tree and help us reach more youngsters. This brought a new awareness to the community and more people could take part. Wherever we received a negative response, the Lord made sure the next one asked would be a positive. We soon had little trees decorated with tags in several areas of the community. It was a great success, but even with that success, we still needed more revenue.

We were trusting the Lord to "open a window" for us, and that is exactly what He did. A friend of ours was managing in-home décor parties at the time. She asked me if I would do parties for her since I had a selling background for so many years. I was a bit reluctant at first, but I knew this was a window of opportunity, so I agreed. I would schedule one or two evening parties during the week and set up parties on weekends. I was working full time during the day and in addition to that would shop for the children. Needless to say there was not much personal time.

During this period of time one of the hospitals sent a press release out to local television channels and the newspaper regarding our ministry. We soon received an invitation to present our story on Channel 13. They would film our delivery of gifts to this particular hospital, interview us for a few minutes and run the segment on their news program. This proved to be a very uncomfortable experience for me, but Charles handled it very well. A newspaper article followed, and soon people in the community who never knew of our endeavor now heard about the plight of some children and contacted us. A number of folks came to our home with gifts and some offered to help wrap. What a wonderful help at a time it was so needed!

To see parents bringing their little children with gifts for the unfortunate children warmed our hearts. One parent remarked their children were learning to share and think of others through our ministry. We began to realize even families in the community were being touched. Not only were the ill and problematic being blessed, the children with a healthy and plentiful life were being taught to reach out to the less fortunate.

Another parent told us, for the first time, their children were learning that life was not always perfect for everyone and here was a way they could reach out to others. Praise God for the lessons that were being taught!

We invited a few of those small children to come help us, and they had a great time. Two of the children had been adopted from Korea, a brother and sister. They were overwhelmed to see rooms totally encompassed with gifts. The look of wonder in the eyes of a child! These children came back three years in a row to sort and wrap items. Their little faces beamed when they, too, received a Santa gift from Santa's Workshop. I believe they will always remember those special times.

December 1992 was coming to a close. Delivery time was upon us. Santa's Workshop was filled with activity and last minute purchases. Doorbell ringing, children singing, elves busy filling cartons with brightly wrapped gifts, made a merry sound. What a sight to see!

Little did we know, a learning experience was about to unfold for us. We were about to experience a truly remarkable moment at one of the hospitals. It was delivery day and several gurneys were bulging at the seams with hundreds of brightly wrapped gifts for the children.

These gurneys were lined up in a corridor along a wall near the elevator. They were going to a storage room on another floor where in just a couple days Santa would be filling his sack with dollies, trucks, stuffed animals, games, book sets and much more and would be presenting a gift at the bedside of each child. Then he would move on to different areas within the hospital bringing joy to many.

We were waiting for the elevator and as the door opened a "man in white" stepped off and began to hold the door for us. Just as we were about to put the first gurney into the elevator, he called out, "wait" and the elevator door closed.

He said, "Are you Mr. and Mrs. Claus?"

Very shyly I answered, "I guess so."

He grinned from ear to ear and said, "Well, what do we have here?" Bubbling over with excitement we began mentioning all the different items inside the packages.

He stopped us and said, "That's not what I meant. Let me tell you what I find in them."

In this corridor stood a doctor holding up several packages, one at a time. As he held one up he said, "This package contains hope and so many children need hope." Then he held another one, and said, "In here could be found the motivation for our little patient to fight harder and hang on for a better day." Then he held another one up and said, "This one tells an ill child they are not alone in their illness, because someone out there cared. This one is full of comfort." (I believe he realized the soft package contained a stuffed animal). Then holding one more gift in his hands he said, "This one is filled with compassion. A stranger feels the hurt of a child." Then he stood back from the gurneys and said, "And all of these packages are filled with love. It is love that wrapped the gift, love that tied the ribbon, and love that attached the bow. It is love for our little patients that brought you here. The greatest gift of all is LOVE!"

By this time our eyes were wet with tears. We had been taught a valuable lesson for all the years to follow by a "man in white". It was not just the item that mattered. It was seeing beyond the gift and the impact it could have on a child's life. It was imperative to channel love to each little soul through the gift given. It was meant to bring the love of God, as well as the love of the donor to each one.

The doctor hugged us both and said, "There is not a medicine in our pharmacy on Christmas day that will bring such comfort and joy as these packages hold. This is the true Spirit of Christmas."

He then began to walk away, then turned around and called out, "By the way, folks, I am the hospital Santa Claus who will be delivering the gifts."

I turned to my husband and remember saying, "Charles, our lives will never be the same again."

They never were because we had been taught the real meaning of the role the Lord asked us to play–to take His love and others to an unfortunate child through a "love gift" given on His birthday. Yes, it is so true, there is no greater gift than love.

As I look back in time, God himself was in the center of that moment. Out of all the many corridors and elevators in that hospital, we were to meet on a certain floor, at a certain elevator and at just the right moment. Who but a loving God could have made a moment in our lives so perfect that even a "man in white" was deeply touched. Truly, there is no greater gift than love!

Chapter 5

Do Unto Others

*"Verily I say unto you, in as much as ye have done it unto one of the least of these, my brethren, ye have done it unto me." **Matthew 25:40***

Toward the end of 1993, a newspaper article drew our attention. This article would advise our community that a decline in donations would cause a well known children's fund to end the giving of toys to children in many local hospitals. The death of a wonderful dedicated man had left the children's fund without a "good will ambassador". The many years of toy giving had brought so many smiles to faces of scared children. An administrator from one of the local hospitals, who had been a recipient of this gracious giving, wondered how this program could ever be replaced. Children in hospitals received toys, not only at Christmas, but year round. We pondered this within our hearts, and wondered if God's hand was extending toward us to be part of the answer.

The weeks were passing swiftly, and Santa's Workshop for Hospitalized Children was abuzz with activity. More and more requests were coming in, not only for the ill youngsters, but the needy as well. How would all this need be met? Once again, the hand of God moved in our direction. We received an invitation from the minister of a little country church to speak to its parishioners about the need in the community and how we were trying to help meet that need. We were welcomed like family that evening and saw smiles resonate on many faces. The response to help with donated gifts was heartwarming and to this very day, these gracious, giving folks are at our side. They have brought joy to many of God's children. Soon after, we heard from another church, also inviting us to speak at a "coffee house" get together. Again, the response was wonderful. Other churches soon followed and invited us to speak at their church services.

What joy to see community coming together. People of all different faiths coming together for a common cause, to reach out to God's little ones of all races, colors and creeds. What a thrill to feel the Lord's love for all his children in such a dimension and to see such caring in action.

Our question, as to how we could meet such need, was answered through community. To see people of all different faiths arriving laden with presents, clothing, wrapping paper and whatever else was needed. Could we replace such a wonderful program that had been bringing so much hope and joy to children in need for so many years? No, we could never replace such giving, but we could help continue it in the way the Lord would lead us. The hospital's concern would be met through our little project and for many years to come. Perhaps one day, we will meet the man who started it all and what a thrill that would be! Looking back, I can see where God was at the center of it all. He would call my husband and me to continue on the good work that had begun in another one of His children.

About this time, we received a note from the parent of a little boy, four years old. The little boy had been in the hospital when he was two and a half years old. He evidently had been blessed with a surprise gift at that time of hospitalization and remembered. He and his Mom had gone shopping for a child aged two who might be in the hospital for Christmas, just like he had experienced.

He wanted us to know he selected a plush "choo-choo train" that made two different sounds when you pushed the buttons. He helped wrap the gift and wanted it to be given to a little boy in need. It brought to mind—"and a child shall lead them." Love expressed from the heart of one child to the heart of another touched our hearts very deeply. We saw this repeated many times over the years from child to child. It is so heartwarming to see faith and love in action!

We were blessed to receive beautiful clothing for those in needy circumstances that warmed heads, hands, feet and hearts. I would like to share the story of a newborn infant at one of the hospitals who was being discharged on Christmas day and received some of this new clothing.

This little soul was dressed in a new nightie, wrapped in a new receiving blanket and its little head covered by a newly knitted baby hat made by a loving person in a little country church. A little key rattle would accompany the new born baby. All items shared through community!

The mother and baby went home via a city transit bus, but before departure, the Mom was delighted to learn that the baby's siblings at home were going to have a Christmas after all. The mother had mentioned to hospital personnel there were no funds to purchase Christmas gifts for the other children at home, but Santa's Workshop supplied lovely gifts for everyone and a Merry Christmas was had by all. We had been blessed to have been a part of this new life and the needs it presented. This was just one of many cases over the years.

To be able to move into needy homes, as well as the other areas, and provide a "moment of joy" was and is heartwarming.

This particular year closed out with the giving of seventeen hundred gifts by family, our elves, friends and community. We had come together as a "body in Christ" and had covered the most children, yet to date. This brings to mind the saying, "Blessed are they who see Christmas through the eyes of a child."

Chapter 6

A Christmas Miracle

"Jesus said, 'With men it is impossible, but not with God; for with God ALL THINGS are possible.'" **Mark 10:27**

The year 1994 arrived with a flurry of activity. Many hours were filled with shopping for the children and trying to find the best sales. We were still on a budget of three to five dollars per gift, and at that time we could find many lovely items in that price range. Also the first segment of the program had to be started early. This was the activity book sets segment.

Charles and I always had the pleasure of doing this part of the project ourselves. With three hundred book sets, each containing five items, it meant purchasing fifteen hundred items consisting of coloring books, readers, tray puzzles, activity fun pads and boxes of crayons. This has always been a costly part of the project; yet the number one request for the hospitals. This is still my biggest contribution to this day. It now takes longer to accomplish this task, as the volume of items is not always available at the time they are sought.

Once this was accomplished, we would move on to dolls, stuffed animals and games with toys to follow. Many long hours were spent coordinating these areas and trying to plan for the needs we would experience. By October we would begin to receive paperwork and calls giving us an idea of the need and the number of children to be served. This practice was followed for many years.

Unbeknown to us, this would be the last year we would be allowed to place our angel tags on the community tree at the store since they had received requests from a number of other agencies and organizations. We were invited to put fifty tags on in place of the one hundred, and we were grateful. However, only twenty five found a place on the tree, and the others were returned to us, allowing other needs in the community to be met. We would always be grateful for the opportunity we were given to make the project more open to the public.

We knew we would need to replace this opportunity with something viable, so we purchased more cute little Christmas trees and put our elves to work cutting out hundreds of angel tags. Each one needed to be written out with age level, boy or girl, which hospital, and a wish list of items with only one to be chosen. This took up many hours, but it was always fun.

We would enlist more businesses to take part, and finally we had trees in many areas of the community, including a large corporation. This meant more gifts would be collected and more folks could participate.

In early December a newspaper article came out stating the Children's Mental and Rehabilitation Center we were serving needed an extra one thousand gifts for their children and families. They were asking for help to fill the waiting list for the "Special Santa" program. This immediately touched our hearts, and we "adopted" one hundred and fifty of those children, meaning we committed to taking Christmas to that number.

We were truly busy at the North Pole as requests flowed in. We even received a call to help a number of poor children in the city, who were not going to have any holiday at all. We were not sure we could accommodate so many extra, but we would trust God, so we committed to covering those youngsters. I can never remember saying no to any request back then. It was just all part of our incredible journey as we leaned ever deeper into the gracious arms of the Lord.

Our goal was to touch the lives of fifteen hundred youngsters, both ill and needy. We were so blessed to cover eighteen hundred and twelve instead. How faithful is our God!

It was nearing delivery time and everyone was excited to load the "sleighs", as we now labeled our vehicles. We made our deliveries to all the hospitals and last Charles and I would deliver to the one hundred and fifty youngsters at the Mental Health Center. It was late afternoon on Christmas Eve when we made our delivery and there were many smiling faces waiting for our arrival. They helped us unload the lovely wrapped gifts, thanked us and wished us a Merry Christmas. We were relieved that all the children in all locations had been covered and Santa's pack would be filled many times over. As we were leaving the Center, a few snowflakes began to tumble to the earth. We were very tired and Charles suggested we return home to freshen up a bit and then go out to dinner. It sounded real good to me.

Immediately upon arriving home the phone rang. I answered to hear the voice on the other end say, "Mrs.

Kinney, this is the Center calling. I know you were just here, but we are in a situation. We just received a call telling us twenty-eight teenagers, all boys, have been removed from their unstable home life and will be arriving here tonight. We didn't anticipate this but these youngsters will not have a gift to open in the morning. We just thought we would check with you and see if you might have anything left for a teenage boy." I advised him we were completely cleaned out at the Workshop. He was concerned that the stores were closing early, and would have a problem getting anything. I felt so bad and helpless that we couldn't help any further.

The receiver had just reclined onto the cradle when I was already in prayer. I told God of the need we had and twenty-eight children would not have anything to open up on His birthday. They had been removed from their homes for safety reasons right on Christmas Eve and stores had closed early. I told Him the entire story, and I now realize that He knew before I did. Even though He knows what is happening in our lives, we are told to ask that we might receive.

Right then, the phone rang again. This time it was a lady at the store where we had collected gifts just a few hours earlier. She said, "Mrs. Kinney, you need to bring your wagon down to the store. You have a number of gifts downstairs". I advised her we had been there, collected the gifts, and in fact just completed all deliveries. She again stated the need for us to return and said more gifts came in during the past few hours.

As Charles came downstairs, I told him we needed to return to the store. This, of course, was the store with the community tree, where he worked.

He had a very puzzled look on his face, but agreed to return. During this period of time, we had not realized that those few snowflakes had grown into heavy snow. The roads were getting slippery and visibility was poor. We arrived at the store and found wrapped gifts lying on the floor in the downstairs. We collected them as quickly as we could, returned home and began checking them out. To our shock and amazement we had thirty-two gifts–thirty of them labeled for teenage boys of various age levels. <u>All boy gifts</u>, just what we needed! Two other gifts were for a baby.

After checking each item, and sticking a few bows here and there, I called the Center, advised them we were on our way with thirty teenage boy gifts. The gentleman on the other end of the phone said, "But you just said you didn't have any gifts left over."

I answered, "We didn't, but God did."

We had just received a miracle! There was no doubt in our minds that a Sovereign Being had put it all together. We were left in awe.

We had started out in what was now a blinding blizzard. The snow was falling heavily, and the lights at intersections could barely be seen. The roads were filling with snow, and the thought passed through my mind that for our safety, we may be should turn back, but something or someone kept us going.

There is a steep incline going up to the residential treatment cottages where the children reside. There are no guard rails, just a drop off on each side. By the time we were half way up the driveway, all we could see was swirling snow everywhere. We lowered the car windows and stuck our heads out the windows trying to see where we were in relation to the edge of the drive.

We made it safely up the hill, and as I looked to my right we were passing the first little cottage where a little face was pressed against the glass pane looking out into the stormy night.

I told my husband about the little child as we made our way around the circle of buildings. We were delivering at the administration building, where again excited, happy people greeted us for the second time.

As we looked around us in the dark of night, the Christmas lights were bursting with color and Christmas carol music was piped in for all to hear. A tranquil moment of beauty filled the air and our hearts. I will always remember the pile of newspapers they had collected should the gifts be unwrapped. They didn't have extra wrapping paper, so newspaper would have to do. Well, they did not need their newspapers as God made sure the gifts were not only correctly age-leveled, but also wrapped in bright colors before we received them. Many tears flowed that holy night as we again received hugs and holiday wishes.

As we returned to our "sleigh" we heard "God bless you" and "a very Merry Christmas!"

I looked up at a few twinkling lights in the sky and I thought about the star that led the wise men to a baby in a manger two thousand years ago. The very originator of that star had now led a man and a woman back to troubled children on earth so their lives might be touched with His light and love and bring glory to His birthday.

I also have wondered to this day what was going through the mind of the little soul whose face pressed against the window pane. Was he wondering if Santa could find him since he wasn't at home? Was he thinking about family and why he couldn't be with them? Was he feeling all alone on a stormy night? Did he feel no one cared and unloved? I will never know for sure nor will he ever know that Mr. & Mrs. Claus passed right by his window. He was loved! God loved him and so did we.

As Mr. & Mrs. Claus crept back home I believe angels accompanied us and kept us safe. We had been sent on a mission and God rewarded us with His Christmas miracle.

As I close this chapter, may we always be a "Santa" in someone else's life:

Making glad the hearts of children

warms their very soul

giving them hope for tomorrow

in a world grown so cold;

helping them to cope with the

"burden of their need"

This we each can do by our

"little caring deed."

Chapter 7

"The Forgotten Ones"

*"For all the law is fulfilled in one word, even in this:
Love your neighbor as yourself." **Galatians 5:14***

Another year was speeding past and only a few weeks remained before another season of "caring and sharing" would fill our agenda. It was 1995 and what a busy year for all of us at Santa's Workshop. Much planning and decision making filled the year's activity. By now, we realized we were the caretakers of the Lord's ever growing project. This would bring forth new strategies to increase community awareness and to raise funds to help meet our increased costs in reaching more and more in need.

This would be our year of introduction to television. The hospitals had brought attention to the project through press releases to the television stations and to the local and city newspapers. They were so excited about the ministry we had that they wanted to share that excitement and also to let the public know what a difference was being made in a needy child's life. Though I was very reluctant to have such publicity, I believed God knew what lay ahead, and He must have felt we needed to journey this pathway.

Therefore, in December of 1995, Charles and I found ourselves on Channel 10 and Channel 13. We were interviewed by Ray Levato on Channel 10 and were featured on Don Alhart's "Bright Spot" segment on Channel 13. This proved to be an enlightening new avenue of telling our story and it made a huge impact on the success of the project. Many people who were unaware of our ministry now learned of our endeavor for the first time, and many responded with inquiries and gifts for the children. Even some businesses collected gifts from their employees. To say the least, we were thrilled!

During the year, I continued setting up in-home House of Lloyd parties on evenings and weekends, sold candy bars, worked full time during the day and spoke at churches and special events in the community.

As all this was occurring, my husband came home one afternoon in February to tell me he was about to lose his job and we were about to lose our main source of income. Those were difficult days, as Charles decided to take early retirement at the employer's suggestion. It was the better way of leaving a twenty-six year employment. The company needed to downsize and Charles was one of those affected. To say our minds were in a whirl was an understatement. Once again our eyes were focused upward to our leader, as our ministry was from Him, and we leaned heavily into His waiting arms. He knew we now had people in several locations truly depending on our help and we knew God would not fail us, ever.

We became even stronger in our faith, and more determined than ever. We knew we had to find another way to earn funds. That avenue proved to be garage sales. We decided we would gather up items we never used or only used very rarely and we would sell them in garage sales. We had a Spring and a Fall sale for many years to come. All proceeds were used to purchase gifts for the children. Over the years, we were able to share many possessions with others, and many new friendships were formed. More folks learned about the need in our community and we received more help from the public. God works in mysterious ways is a saying from way back and it is very true.

During this time we learned from the hospitals that our giving was being extended throughout areas of the hospitals including the Blood Draw Station and Surgical

Center. Frightened children at the Blood Draw Station were distracted from the procedure by a stuffed animal or toy. This helped everyone involved including the nurses. What brought tears to our eyes was learning that little souls on gurneys to the Operating Room cuddled their "new friend" (new stuffed animal) enroute. They were comforted by their "new friend" and didn't feel alone. This truly made our hearts leap with joy to think we were there in spirit even on their way to surgery. We would also be active in bringing joy to children with sickle cell anemia and hemophilia, as these were chronic patients, who needed an extra dose of love as well as children dealing with domestic abuse. Would we have ever imagined reaching out to so many children in so many situations? Never, in a million years, but the Lord had a plan and we would go where we were led, and we would make a difference in His name.

At this point in time, we would be contacted by the hospital who worked diligently with the children so disabled they were known as "the forgotten ones". This now meant we were working with four hospitals. We agreed to bring Christmas to those hurting souls, despite my husband's job loss. They had special needs, so we alone did their shopping.

I remember standing in the toy aisles in the stores, crying, as we looked for just the right item for a totally disabled child. A little two year old girl needed a mobile to hang above her bed. Since she didn't have the freedom of movement, she could look at a moving mobile. We chose a musical one so she would hear pretty music, especially if we could find one with nursery rhymes.

An immobile fourteen year old boy wished to have some wall hangings such as sport's star posters. I would ask God to lead us to a special place to get those and He did.

A little three year old boy also needed a mobile above his bed and others wished for the comfort of a simple stuffed animal.

We would never forget the eighteen year old girl so mentally injured that the hospital thought a xylophone would be helpful to her as she only had use of her hands. This request came right before Christmas and Charles and I visited store after store trying to find one. We were about to give up searching, when at the very last store we visited, one small one laid on a shelf. We grabbed that one quickly. It was probably not exactly what was hoped for but it was a xylophone anyway.

This brings me back to the question I mentioned earlier in the book. The question we have so often been asked, "Why do you continue to do this!" I wonder if you still need an answer. It is my hope and prayer that you do not need an answer, but that the answer is clear.

"The forgotten ones" are not only totally disabled, but can be children of horrible mental and physical abuse. They can be children with great emotional unbalance and children signed over by parents who have lost total control of their lives. They can be children abandoned by their very loved ones and children who only ask to be loved. Are we not here to love others? Have we not been placed on earth to make a difference in another human being's life? Do we have to know that person or child? No, we do not; all we have to know is there is a need to be met, and that need can be met by channeling God's love to one another to meet the fulfillment of the law: "Love thy neighbor as thyself." What a wonderful world we could realize if we all would, "come and see; then go and do."

Yes, we were blessed abundantly despite our main loss of income and 2,180 children had a "bit of Christmas" and all were touched by love.

Chapter 8

"You're All Mine"

"Beware that you do not look down on any of these little ones, for I tell you that in Heaven their angels are always in the presence of my heavenly Father." Matthew 18:10

I share my daydream with you

For it always starts the same

It rests deep within my soul

It cries out; yet has no name.

It tugs at my very heart string

It calls to me all night long

If only pain and suffering would vanish

And be replaced in a child's life with song.

These words express the feelings that have lived within my being for many years of this ministry. To witness pain in the face of a child and feel it through the sadness in their eyes is something very hurtful that one does not forget. Though weeks pass by swiftly and years come and go, the daydream remains the same.

Why do I call it a daydream? Because it is just that – a daydream. It is not a reality of the harshness of life; it is only a wish of the heart.

This year of 1996 would teach us a lesson about the reality of life, that even in its most harsh moments, we can participate in the softening of, and the sharing in, of one's suffering.

We were now learning of some life threatening situations that a few of the children were experiencing. We wondered how we could interact with these children on an even deeper level. We decided on **very large** stuffed animals we would call "specials". We would select beautiful , very large puppies, soft bodied dollies, teddy bears and especially any large angel bears we could find. These were costly to purchase and above our budgeted amount, but the joy and comfort they would bring to a critically ill or dying child had no price tag. They would not be wrapped and would accompany us to the hospitals apart from the wrapped gifts. They always have made a wonderful "gift of hope" for all children.

I would like to share with you the special role these "specials" have played in a child's life over the years.

In one of the local hospitals we were serving, a sweet little girl had been valiantly fighting a battle with leukemia. Sadly, she was losing her fight with the vicious disease, and her story reached our community through the newspapers. The sadness we felt for this little soul was overwhelming. We selected a beautiful white angel bear for her and since she was too ill for us to visit her, we could only pass it on to her nurse. The nurse took the angel bear into her and rested it beside her. At this point in time the little girl was too weak to even sit up and was propped up by pillows. A couple nights later we would receive a phone call telling us of her passing.

She had only enjoyed her "angel friend" a couple of days, but before she was called into the "hall of eternity", here is the story as related to us.

After having placed the angel bear at her side, the nurse was almost into the hospital corridor, when she thought she heard a murmur. She re-entered the room only to find this terribly weakened child sitting up in bed, unsupported, rocking the angel bear back and forth in her little arms, saying "You're all mine, you're all mine".

The nurse told us she nearly broke down before the child. Where had she found such strength where there appeared to be no strength? I will let you, the reader, decide.

As this story was told to me via phone I began sobbing. The voice on the other end said, "Mrs. Kinney, I didn't call you to upset you and make you cry. I called you to let you know of the joy and comfort you brought to a dying child. Please don't cry; instead smile. Smile for the joy that was brought her way and for the pain she no longer knows."

Over the years the story of that little girl has lived on in my heart and soul. Though occasionally, a tear still wets the eye, I must smile. She touched our lives and a community with her smile and bubbly personality. For one man, especially, she changed the direction of his life. Today he operates a toy fund that is backed by corporations, and thousands more children, both ill and needy, are remembered with gifts all year long. Would you not call that a miracle? Since her death, this little girls' parents have purchased hundreds of gifts over the years for other ill youngsters.

Our Lord sends sunlight even through the darkest days of life. If we could only believe in His sunlight, and hold on to it in our daily lives, then share that light with others, how much more wonderful life would be for all of us. The peace we all could realize and the love we all could experience would be incredible. He does have a purpose for us, not only in living, but also in death.

Another child who comes to mind was lying in the Burn Unit in another hospital. This child had been severely burned over much of its little body. We were delivering gifts that day, along with our "specials". I was standing in the corridor with a beautiful, very large teddy bear in my arms. A nurse passed by me, then looked back at me, returned to where I was standing and asked me if that bear was for anyone special. I told her it was meant for a child in distress or in a critical situation. She said, "Give me the bear quickly. We have a child down this hall in our Burn Unit fighting for life. Just, maybe, this bear will make a difference, and the child will find the strength to fight."

She grabbed the bear out of my arms and ran down the hallway, then turned around and shouted, "We need more than this bear, we need help from the man upstairs." Again, the tears fell as I stood praying in a hospital corridor for a stranger's child who lay in incredible pain. Was that child meant to have a special bear at its side? Yes! Was that nurse meant to meet me in that very corridor of the Burn Unit and take a large comforting animal to comfort a child in such pain? Was I meant to be in that exact corridor at that very moment? To this very day, my answer is a resounding yes! My husband was helping unload that day and missed that special moment in time, but a loving God decided to share it with me.

A small child can literally cuddle their little being into a very large stuffed animal. It can become a haven for them to rest **into** and share their circumstance with "their best friend". The hope, comfort and joy these very large animals bring to an ill and dying child is immeasurable. Only God knows the final impact they make. We all need love, but these little ones need an even greater love, for they do not fully understand all that lies ahead for them. They cry in fear of the unknown. This is especially true of cancer patients.

Recently I spoke with a retired nurse who has worked with cancer children in Virginia for many years. She retired a few years ago, but her memories of suffering children drew her back out of retirement and she is now a volunteer at the same hospital. She now sits for hours at their bedside trying to bring a smile and a little hope to each one. She can't escape hearing the crying of these children as they ask what is going to happen to them. They are frightened so she holds their hand, comforts them, reads them a story, and asks nothing in return. This lady is a blessing, indeed, and the children need her.

Yes, I have a daydream that lives within me, and so it shall be. That daydream fills me with hope for a better tomorrow. One day, my daydream will no longer exist, for it will become reality. Reality in a beautiful place beyond the veil, when pain and suffering will no longer have its hold on adult or child. Perhaps, as we have our first peek at a place called Heaven, we also will be able to speak those same words, "You're all mine, you're all mine".

Chapter 9

Jesus Loves the Little Children

*"Children are a gift from the Lord; they are
a reward from him."* **Psalm 127:3**

Once again the signs of Autumn were upon us. The honking of wild geese, the peeping of crickets, cool breezes and vibrant colors filled the air with sound and beauty. This meant our workshop days were around the corner. It was 1997 and the year had been filled with planning strategies, year round gift shopping, seeking additional "elves" and community support.

On the strategy end, we decided to add decorated wreaths along with our decorated trees which would give us more visibility in the community. We would make a change in our candy program and switch over to Niagara Chocolates Wholesaler where we would earn fifty percent of sales. This would give us a little boost on that end. Added to that strategy was a Spring and Fall garage sale with all proceeds going to the children. Once again, we were on our way to bringing smiles to many little faces.

In November, we received notification from the hospital known for aiding cancer children that we would no longer need to wrap their gifts of toys, games, dolls, and stuffed animals. The book sets of activities would continue to be wrapped. The reason for the change was very understandable. Children were more acutely ill and they also were seeing more disabled children with bodily limitations. There was no way Santa himself could select the appropriate gift for each child. The selections would need the expertise of hospital personnel. This, of course, made things a bit easier for us also. It meant less wrapping paper to purchase along with bows and ribbon. It worked out fine on both ends, and the processing of their gifts went very smoothly. The remaining hospitals stayed with brightly wrapped packages.

Around this time we received a call from a nursery school teacher in another county who had learned of our giving via television. She saw our segment on one of the channels and felt led to become a part of that giving. She had a good size class of "little folk", who, she believed, could have a learning experience about sharing with unfortunate children. We were thrilled to have her interest and participation. I would take angel tags to her and she would have each child select a tag. They would take it home to their parents with a note from the teacher asking for only **one** gift. The angel tag was returned with the appropriate gift circled on the tag. All gifts were wrapped. What a wonderful experience this proved to be, working with such little tots and seeing the wonder in their eyes. At one point they gave ninety gifts to the children, three times what was expected. They were so excited when I arrived to pick up the gifts. They would sit in a large circle with their little legs crossed while I told them about Santa's Workshop. Some of the littlest ones believed I came from the North Pole and I was truly Santa's helper. When I told them they all were my "little elves" they would cheer and clap their hands.

Yes, Jesus loves the little children!

What wonderful memories of those special times! They would play the role of "elves" for several years until a number of the children's Dads were called to war, and home life changed.

Activity was well under way at Santa's Workshop. One snowy evening, as we were processing requests our doorbell rang. A lady stood there with a large bag of games. She had just come from the store shopping for the children. She had never seen the project in action before, so her eyes lit up when she saw all the beautifully wrapped gifts. She was in total amazement! We chatted a few moments and I thanked her for caring and sharing.

She then said, "I will be back soon with more items."

I advised her she had done more than enough and we were grateful.

She said, "I have to do this!"

She went out into a snowy night and I watched the lights of her vehicle fade into the dark of the night.

About an hour later the doorbell rang again. The same lady stood at the door with another huge bag full of toys and more games. I asked her into the living room where she told her story.

A few years earlier she had been watching the news on television when an orphanage across the waters was showing little babies and toddlers who had been orphaned and had been put up for adoption. She saw one little boy standing up in the crib with a very disfigured face, crying. He had been born with a cleft palate.

She told her husband, "There is our son."

They began adoption proceedings and after quite a period of time, money and protocol this little orphan arrived in America. They could not have loved a biological child any more than they loved that orphaned child. She told us of numerous surgeries he had been through to correct the disfigurement, and would still need more.

She said to us, "I have to tell you, each time he went in for surgery a little toy laid on his bed. I can never forget the joy and comfort it brought him. When I heard about this project, I had to come. I had to bring the children gifts on behalf of my little son. He still has surgeries ahead of him; his little face will never be perfect, but it will be better. At least he will be able to eat easier and know what solid food is like and for that we are thankful."

We admired this lady so much and tears filled my eyes as I hugged her and wished their little orphaned boy our very best. Such love oozed from this lady as she stood there thanking Charles and myself for all we were doing for hurting children.

She looked at us and said, "It must be difficult financially for you. We are really hurting in that area, due to so many surgeries, but we're not hurting to the point we can't give back. That's why I stand here tonight, to give back in thankfulness for our son."

A lesson to be learned? I would say, definitely! Here was a mother, who loved a stranger's child from across the world so much, that she would give all of what she had to provide a home and future for this little God created soul. She only wanted him to be loved and accepted just as he was–to see the real little boy beyond the flaws. Isn't that our hope also?

I believe God sent her to our home so we would be encouraged to continue on and not grow weary. She was an inspiration to us that snowy night and I will always remember her story and her kindness. The Lord had spoken to our hearts once again that we had so much to be thankful for and it was His will that we continue on the incredible journey He would lay before us. We also learned Jesus so loves his little orphans.

Santa's Workshop was once again very blessed by all who crossed our pathway. Together as a "body in Christ" we brightened the lives of 2,836 children. This was a dream come true for all of us; and the largest number of gifts to date. The Lord had led our pathways once again; yet so much more lay ahead–more than we could have ever imagined!

Chapter 10

The Communion of Community

"And God is able to make all grace abound toward you; that ye, always having all sufficiency **in all things**, *may abound to every good work." 2 Corinthians 9:8*

The scriptures reinforce our need to depend on a higher power that our abundance might be full. We are told by His wondrous grace flowing toward us, we shall have all we need. This applies to every good work on earth. His storehouse of supply has no end – it is always there, waiting for each of us to draw upon it. When we are in His will, the door will never be closed to us and we can enter into and draw upon his riches day and night.

The Lord's wondrous grace flowed like a river in 1998, in a way that made it the most event filled year of our ministry, at that point in time. Right from the beginning of the year there seemed to be a "static" in the air at Santa's Workshop for Hospitalized Children. We were receiving more phone calls than ever before. Not just calls of inquiry, but calls offering help. Folks in the community wanting to know how they could help touch a child's life for the holidays.

The Visiting Nurse Service in our community called to say they would love to have angel tags and would distribute them among personnel. This generous offer provided us with a car load of beautiful gifts, all unexpected.

Next, two hairdressers in a nearby county asked for decorated trees for their beauty salons and they would offer their customers the opportunity to select a tag for a child. This was a wonderful idea, and more gifts poured in.

We added a new candy wholesaler to our candy business who offered variety boxes of candy. This eliminated much work for us and made our candy purchasers happy. In March of that year, we had a candy bar fundraiser that was very successful. Sixteen businesses participated, along with friends and family, and God blessed our efforts.

In the summer months I became hostess for another in-home party company. I hosted several parties, made new friends, and got the word out about the children. Our support was growing rapidly, as neighbor told neighbor about our ministry.

In July we put on a fundraiser at an American Legion hall in our community. We had displays of Avon products, in-home products, candy, baked food sale, raffle, and prize drawing every half hour. Some of the delicious baked goods were donated by a bakery in our community and the remainder by friends.

On the candy end, we brought in candy fromWashington state, so the community would have something a little different from the candy we sold.

The raffle drawing was to raise funds for a young lad in the community who was suffering with leukemia and desperately needed a bone marrow transplant. Much hard work and long hours of planning went into that fundraiser.

In August, a phone call left us stunned! A gentleman from a local newspaper advised us we had been nominated along with five other folks for the Citizen of the Year Award. This is an award given for volunteer community service where other lives are touched by that service. We were shocked to learn that we were going to be the recipients of that award. What an honor to receive such community respect and support! It is something I will forever cherish and it meant a great deal to Charles.

In September, as we were planning our Fall garage sale, we received an invitation from the Council of Churches in our area to speak at their upcoming meeting. We were happy to do so, and were given a marvelous opportunity to share "our story" with them.

These wonderful, caring people truly understood what our ministry was about, and they began community support of our endeavor. They have been there for us year after year and I am very humbled. A number of these gracious folks from all different churches bring gifts, sort, and help wrap to this very day. This loyal support helps us reach out to many more youngsters in need. God's storehouse of supply was opening wide in a number of different facets.

Later in the month, we would advertise a Fall garage sale advising all proceeds going to the purchase of gifts for the children. God blessed us again, as hundreds of folks browsed and purchased items. New friendships evolved and more folks spread the word. It was fascinating to see how God was touching lives within our community.

This particular year, as the holiday approached, we received an urgent request for donations from a community center in a nearby county. This center feeds and helps clothe

the needy in their area. They do a great job in helping others and we were pleased to answer their request for help with an affirmative. We are a part of their community service to this day.

At this point in time, we had grown from one hospital in 1989 to four hospitals, a mental health center, and now a community center. This called for thousands of gifts and God's storehouse was opened and His awesome grace flowed toward us.

And then another call–this time from the Salvation Army asking us for new toys. We said we would share all that we were receiving, and after filling thousands of requests, we had one hundred thirty-five new toys left over. Does this not remind you of the loaves and fishes story in the Bible? From the Lord's storehouse of supply we were able to cover every little child in all different locations with a "love gift" from Santa. As the sleighs were loaded that December, 3,398 ill and needy children had a moment of joy.

That joy was made possible through a "team effort"–God and community. From tots in a daycare, from customers in beauty salons, from visiting nurses, to community at fundraisers, we were a team under the watchful eye of the Master.

What did the scripture say? I believe it stated, "That, you, always having all sufficiency in **all things**, may abound to every good work."

Praise and honor to our Lord!

From the Heart of a Child

I'm just a "little person" whom
you have yet to meet
I'm someone's little playmate
who lives down the street.
Recently I learned I would not be
home on Christmas Day
Not feeling very "chipper", the
hospital would be my stay.

A light went out when I thought
about my Christmas tree
And things were looking pretty
bleak for Mom, Dad and me.
But then on Christmas morning,
I felt movement on my bed
With one eye awakening, I saw a
jolly, bearded man in red.

He was carefully selecting lovely
gifts from a laden sack
For a "special moment" I did not
feel the pain within my back.
A light returned within me; I felt
love and warmth abound
As quietly he stole away; his steps
making very little sound.

I was as excited as if they had
been under my own tree
As I gazed upon my truck and a
knitted hat made just for me.
And a little girl across the hall
just shouted out with glee
She received a sailor doll and dishes
to take dolly out to tea.

I know that you, dear friend, played a special part

In bringing joy to little folk – it

deeply touched my heart.

Perhaps one day, chance will plan

that you and I shall meet

For I might be the new neighbor

who lives just down the street.

With deepest thanks,

Florence B. Kinney

Chapter 11

Solely By His Grace

*"As each one has received a gift, minister it one to another, as good stewards of the manifold grace of God." **1 Peter 4:10***

There is a saying that no man is an island, and no one walks alone. Yet, in this world, there are those who feel they are an island and they truly feel they are alone. I cannot think of a more appropriate Bible verse for the year 1999, than the verse which opens this Chapter.

We each have a **gift to give**, that is **ordained** of God, and it is our responsibility to minister that gift to one another. The gifts of love, hope, compassion and charity can turn a life around. These **God given gifts** bring sunlight into the darkness and make a difference for **all** involved.

This is exactly what Santa's Workshop for Hospitalized Children experienced this particular year. The Spirit of God moved through our community in a miraculous way. Neighbor was telling neighbor and children in schools were being given the opportunity to share with another less fortunate child. They responded with many "gifts of love." Even a few notes accompanied some gifts and we sent those notes along with the gift.

Young children volunteered their time to sort and wrap gifts. I remember the fun they had interacting with each other. Some community organizations began offering assistance in whatever way it was needed. Individuals sent notes of encouragement and at times a small monetary gift asking if we would shop for them, since we knew the needs requested. Kindness from the heart, I would say.

Senior citizens began knitting hats, scarves and mittens for the needy, a practice which continues blessing youngsters to this very day. One lady in our community has knitted nearly three thousand such items. Isn't it incredible what even one human being can accomplish in a life time? It is truly amazing, and to think all this "team effort" exists solely through and by the wondrous **Grace of God.**

In Chapter X, I spoke of the "Communion of Community" and it seemed to explode this year in several areas. Several newspaper articles were written about the workshop and our efforts to brighten lives. Our ministry began to soar on the wings of eagles. Surely the Master of it all smiled down upon us and knew "it was good."

By fall, we would learn of an increase in need in another area. In addition to serving several hospitals, a Mental Health Center and an area Community Center, we would add another agency to our list. We would receive an inquiry from a non-profit organization which served as a support system helping children and their families cope with serious illness, death and separation due to foster placement.

This service had serviced eight thousand youngsters in our Finger Lakes region and surrounding counties for fifteen years. This organization worked with children in foster homes who felt unloved by their biological family. Some children had lost a sibling to death and had problems coping with loss. Feelings of fear, guilt, sadness, and anger had raised havoc in their lives and they were confused about their well being. We were asked if we could share our bounty with these children. We knew the Lord was moving his Spirit in a huge way upon all of us, and Santa's Workshop agreed to help.

Through the Lord's grace and from his storehouse of supply, we covered two hundred fifteen of these less fortunate children with a "bit of Christmas."

The Child Psychologist of this organization came to our workshop that December and collected the lovely gifts of Ty Beanie Babies, toys, games and books, all geared to appropriate age level. What a grateful doctor left our home that day!

We were now receiving more and more requests for angel tags. This included even a bakery, bank, again several hair salons, Visiting Nurse, churches, and once again the Co-op Nursery, who this time around, donated one hundred gifts. Even a mini grocery store collected gifts for us through a tagged wreath. This was in addition to the local businesses who had accepted decorated mini trees and those selling our candy bars to their customers and employees. What a "Communion of Community" ministering time, talent and gifts all shared solely through the mighty grace of a mighty God.

Delivery time had arrived once again. This year, upon arriving at one of the hospitals, which by the way, would grab up our knitted baby hats as soon as they were delivered, had a family of siblings, all suffering from the same serious disease. They were being treated as outpatients. This family was totally depleted of funds due to medical bills. Insurance had run its course, so there would not be any Christmas at their home. The parents were heavily burdened in mind and heart, and didn't know how to tell these sick youngsters that Santa would not be coming this year.

The hospital personnel advised Charles and I of this situation upon our arrival. Our hearts were deeply touched. We advised the lady speaking to us to select several appropriate gifts tagged for their age level. We told her to make sure these children received a visit from Santa, and we were to remain anonymous.

These gifts were selected immediately before department heads arrived to select the gifts they needed for the little ones in their units.

We were advised later on those parents rested their heads in their hands and sobbed uncontrollably. They had been beaten down by adversity, but now lifted up in hope and love. They could not believe that strangers cared about them. I hope they came to realize that a loving God cared also and was smiling down on each of them.

Shortly thereafter, a lady called our name and we turned to see a smiling face coming toward us. This lady shook our hands and said, "I heard you were coming today and I had to speak with you." She was in charge of their Children's Psychiatric Ward. She explained to us they had a little seven year old boy there, who had been so abused, he no longer would speak. There was no verbal communication with anyone, nor would he see anyone from the outside world. This little child had been kicked around repeatedly like you would kick a football. He had lost all sense of worth and felt alone. She asked if we would share a few toys with him. She didn't know if he would ever communicate again or trust anyone again.

Just maybe, he would realize, hopefully, that someone did care about him in the outside world. With tears in our eyes, and much sadness in our hearts, we helped select toys such as a truck, hot wheels–toys appropriate for a little boy. She took them from us quickly, hugged us, and said, "Let's hope and pray these make a difference." Charles and I not only sent that little soul toys, but our prayers as well. We asked her to give him a hug from us and I'm sure she did. I think of that child to this day and I have always wondered if his life had been destroyed forever by human cruelty. I pray he was able to understand that others did care and loved him from afar.

This exciting year twenty-eight cartons of new store purchased and lovingly knitted pieces of clothing would be distributed along with toys, games, stuffed animals and five hundred forty-four activity book sets. All totaled, 3,454 "gifts of love" were distributed to several locations, delighting the hearts of many.

The children were delighted, but so were we. We knew every ray of hope, every strength provided, every blessing we left behind was made possible solely by and through the Grace of a loving God.

Chapter 12

The Chosen

"Ye have not chosen me, but I have chosen you, and ordained you, that ye should go and bring forth fruit, and that your fruit should remain: that whatsoever ye shall ask the Father in my name, he may give it you." **John 15:16**

What **powerful words** from our Lord! He makes clear we did not choose Him; instead He chose us from the very beginning of our existence. We all are His children and He has endowed us with purpose. From the moment we arrived on earth, God placed "fruitful" gifts within us. However, it is our choice whether to accept those gifts or reject them. The keyword here is **OBEDIENCE!**

You may wonder why I open this chapter with this particular message. My answer is this: for the past twenty-two years of my life, and fourteen years of my husband's life, the Lord sent His "chosen" to help us carry out our ministry for His less fortunate children. He called them "chosen"; we called them our "elves".

In 1990, when we were **called** to this ministry, we asked, "Why us?" We were just everyday folks living the "norm of life." Why would the Lord ask us to put the "norm" of our lives aside to focus on the needs of others? We were not ready to change our life style, so we answered in the negative. In order for God to fulfill His plan for our lives, He "chose" a newspaper reporter we had never met to change our minds and help us realize our focus was not where it was supposed to be. **When we turned to God**, He "chose" us to be His "emissaries" for the ill and needy children in this world. **When we became OBEDIENT** to His will for our lives, He raised us up on eagle wings and took us to heights we would never have experienced. I cannot answer the question, why us, but one day, as I kneel before His majestic presence, I know He will answer my question.

This I do know: as His children, we are special in His eyes and heart. Because we are special in His sight, we have been personally and individually "chosen" to be His representatives and witnesses in the world. When we become obedient to His "calling" for our lives, then we shall truly know the **abundant life** He planned for us from the very beginning.

The nineties had come and gone. A new century lay before us. It was the year 2000 and the "norm" for us was under way with strategy planning, year round shopping, hosting in-home parties and speaking at various functions. As Fall approached, we began receiving calls from the community. Some were from folks we had not heard from before. One such lady called to say she had two large cartons full of knitted items for children. She had wondered who she would give them to and also **why she felt led** to continue knitting despite two cartons already full. She then heard of our ministry and said she **knew immediately** that she had knitted all those beautiful items for us. Was this lady "chosen?" Indeed! She had been called and she willingly obeyed. Many little folk were warmed that winter through the God given gift she had been given with the wonderful use of her hands.

Much fruit was produced and that type of fruit is being produced year after year in this ministry. We have a number of senior citizens who have been "chosen" to knit for the children each and every year. The colors are as beautiful as any rainbow I have ever seen. Solid colors, mixed colors –

infant, small, medium and large sizes in hats and mittens. Scarves of all colors and sizes filled cartons along with baby booties and gorgeous baby blankets. These beautiful items lift the morale of a less fortunate child as well as warm their heart and body. Most importantly, love is sealed into every stitch and love is what it is all about. These gracious folks are a part of our "elf family"; "chosen" by the Master.

Others God has "chosen" to be part of our "elf family" purchase gifts, give of their time and talent in sorting, sizing, wrapping, processing requests, helping load "sleighs", and in whatever way they can help. I would like to mention the "elves" who have worked with us late into the night and even in the early morning hours, helping us complete the delivery that would be due just a few hours later. This was done cheerfully and without complaint. It is not an easy choice to drive late at night in a snow storm to a Workshop that is falling behind on their time schedule. Again, these folks were "chosen" to help us complete the task at hand, and the Lord kept each one safe in their travels.

In the Fall of this particular year, the hospitals and the Mental Health Center were adding books of all age levels to their wish lists, advising us they were truly needed. Children in hospital beds could pass time by reading a story.

Children in rehab, who were in traction with a broken leg or hip would love a book to read. Children in cottages might enjoy reading to each other, encouraging interaction.

Since Charles and I would already purchase three hundred plus Golden books for the activity sets, our budget would not allow any further funds for books. Therefore, we added them as suggestions to our tags and outgoing wish lists. We received a few from the public, but we would need many more. And, then came a phone call from our local library telling us they had some small books they no longer would be using. They were children's books, and they would offer them to us if we could use them. We were so appreciative to receive thirty-four books. This was the only time we received their donations, but it was perfectly timed.

Still there was a big gap between what we had received and what we needed. Right about this time, a lady brought her two children to our workshop, offering to wrap book sets. They had heard about our ministry from others and needed to see what it was all about. They were amazed to see rooms totally consumed with items for the children and their hearts were touched. Pictures were taken so others could see the magnitude of the project, as they did not live in our community, but rather a number of miles away. This lady did not know of the need we had at this particular time; she was caught up in the hustle of activity on that particular day and had a wonderful time wrapping gifts with her children.

A few days later, a phone call from this lady would make our hearts leap for joy. She would share her story with us: **unbeknown to us,** she was a book merchandiser in several large stores in the surrounding area. It was her job to keep new children's books on store shelves. After a certain period of time, books that were not selling would be removed. Some would be literally destroyed; in other words, thrown away in store dumpsters. Others would be cartoned and returned to the distributor.

On this particular day, she told us she was about to destroy a large number of new books from the various locations she serviced, when a thought passed through her mind, *"why are you destroying books that children could be reading?"* She said she abruptly stopped destroying the books. She felt led to seek permission from the distributors to share them with a charitable cause. She received permission from some of the distributors to share these wonderful storybooks. Needless to say, her call was to ask us if we could use **hundreds** of new books in our ministry—brand new books off store shelves. I jumped for joy and was so excited! She advised we would need to transport them to Santa's Workshop since she had a very small vehicle. We had a large wagon at the time that was perfect for transporting. We made several trips to her home, each time filling "our sleigh" to capacity. The wish for **all age levels** to have books was met. Hundreds of children enjoyed a new book for Christmas.

Was this lady "chosen" to meet a need we had at the Workshop? Was she tapped on the shoulder on this particular day by divine interception and advised not to destroy, but rather to share? We had no doubt at all that she had been truly "chosen" to join our "elf family" and make glad the heart of a child.

Once again another need was met, and once again, God's love and light shone through another year of caring and sharing.

Each and every "elf" the Lord has sent to us over these many years has helped this ministry to continue blessing others. Whether you were an "elf" for one hour, one day, many days or many years, may you know in reading this chapter, you will be forever remembered by Mr. & Mrs.

Claus. You answered the Lord's call; you responded to the tap on your shoulder and you did not question. You came; you gave and you touched the hearts of thousands of His little children. You helped us take God's love to those who needed to feel loved. We will always be grateful for your love, your kindness and your generosity. Now, may His precious love flow toward you and shower you with His blessings, as you have been a blessing to others.

I would like to close this chapter with this thought: As we journey through life, people from all walks of life, people of all different faiths and people searching for a purpose, will cross our pathway. They come into the main stream of our existence, sometimes only for a fleeting moment; sometimes for many years. They seek a higher calling for their lives, but are afraid to step beyond their comfort zone. In the sad and havoc world we live in today, we must seek God's will for our lives and ask Him to move us forward, leaving our comfort zone behind. We cannot be fruitful, as the Scripture for this chapter states, and live in a shell. We were created to serve God and each other. Not one person was ever created without a purpose for their life. If we focus upward, we will find that purpose. We will be fruitful and blessings from Heaven will be ours.

The "fruits" of Santa's Workshop will forever remain in the hearts of many. May the candle the Lord lit for this ministry twenty-two years ago never be extinguished! May the candle of love, hope, faith and compassion burn somewhere, somehow, by someone who will receive "the calling" to keep His love and light forever flowing toward His "little ones" everywhere.

Chapter 13

The Littlest Angel

"Now we see things imperfectly, like puzzling reflections in a mirror, but then we see everything with perfect clarity. All that I know now is partial and incomplete, but then I will know everything completely, just as God now knows me completely." **I Corinthians 13:12**

The Fall of 2001 arrived in all its glorious color. A new crispness filled the air. The holidays were upon us and soon the buzz of activity would be heard at Santa's Workshop for Hospitalized Children.

Paperwork containing wish lists and phone calls to verify needs and numbers had already been received. During the year we added our local power plant to our candy list of participants. A local florist who knew of our ministry called to offer us some lovely items they were pulling from their stock due to non-sales. Items such as trolls, which were very popular then, large stuffed animals and a few small dolls came our way. Even wonderful baby items were donated. How grateful we were to receive such kindness!

This particular Fall we would be advised by another local hospital that we would no longer need to wrap all gifts. Again, we were told, due to allergies, asthma and other respiratory problems along with certain disabilities, it was necessary for the hospital personnel to make the final selection of gifts. This way each child was certain to receive a gift they could enjoy. All activity sets would still be wrapped and are to this very day.

Once again, we would seek the support of community with garage sales, candy fundraiser, and tagged wreaths and trees as need spiraled upward. We would accept speaking invitations in hope of touching more hearts, enabling us to reach out to more less fortunate children.

Again this year we would be contacted by the hospital, which was "home" to the "forgotten children." These little folk only saw a hospital room, corridor, doctors and nurses. They were children of limited motion with serious disabilities, who truly suffered the adversities of life. This particular year we would have a little nine month old baby and a one year old on our list. The nine month old baby would need some baby toys and a mobile for its crib. We found a teddy bear mobile that would light up when a button was pressed and a little toy to place in the crib. For the one year old, a talking toy or animal was suggested. We were able to find a talking monkey this child could see and hear, as very limited mobility was involved.

A six year old was unable to move below the neck, so no play-with-action toy could be given. This child loved the Power Rangers, so videos were suggested and anything where this child could learn about animals. Two nine year old children needed a **toy** to attach to the bed rail. We selected a small lamb for one and a small lion for the other. A twelve year old wished for a colorful poster for the wall. Because of lack of movement, this child could only lie flat and stare at the poster hour after hour, day after day.

Perhaps you can understand why I wept standing in toy aisles, purchasing items for the correct age level of the older children. They would receive items normally selected for babies and toddlers. This pulled at our hearts more than once. It brought to mind how **thankful** we should be even **for the tiniest gifts of life**. A smile, a hug, a sunbeam ray, a budding flower at "morn" of day all call for a grateful heart.

There are children who would thrill to see a rainbow after the rain and cannot see. There are paralyzed children who yearn to play ball and cannot. There are children who cry out to be loved and are not. There are children who know hunger, not just across the waters, but right here at home and have not. There are children horribly abused and left with scars for a lifetime. Yes, my husband and I saw and heard of much sadness over the years.

As I mentioned earlier in this book, to see such hurt in a child's eyes is a memory never forgotten. It taught us to remember that the grass is not always greener on the other side.

This December, as we filled Santa's sack over and over again,

3,500 youngsters received a "love gift" on our Savior's birthday. Mr. & Mrs. Claus were deeply moved and touched by the courage and strength of the youngsters fighting adversity in their lives. They set an example for each one of us, who take so much for granted. They make the complaints we have about life seem very small; in fact, we should not complain at all.

I will share one such example with you. Charles and I arrived at this same hospital to deliver the children's gifts, that is the special needs gifts. As prepared as I thought I was, I soon learned one is never prepared to see such adversity. One must be very strong emotionally, and I am not that person. My husband, being much stronger, decided it would be best if he delivered the gifts since I felt I could not handle seeing these little ones so impaired. He suggested I take the elevator down to a lower level and visit a friend who was a patient there.

I stepped onto the elevator, pushed the proper floor button which lit up. The elevator began moving when I noticed another lighted floor button. I just figured someone else was waiting for the elevator. However, the elevator proceeded to the other signaled floor. The door opened; yet, no one was waiting. Instead, I found myself gazing at a heart wrenching sight. A beautiful little girl with long golden blonde hair, an angelic face, dressed in powder blue, lay by the nurses' station propped up on a hospital bed. Her little body was wrenching convulsively from head to foot. Her little arms were flailing outward; her head bobbing back and forth, up and down. The first words that crossed my mind were "little angel." Her little head was cupped in the nurse's hand as the nurse tried desperately to place a straw through her lips to moisten her mouth with a bit of liquid.

As the elevator door finally closed, I remember crying out, "Dear God, why?" I then began to slide downward toward the elevator floor. I do not clearly remember the next few moments, but somehow, or with the help of someone, I found myself standing in a hospital corridor sobbing uncontrollably. Charles would find me a short time later. He took me outside in the hospital yard. We would sit on a bench, his arms encircling a trembling body. I tried to explain what I had witnessed. He then told me we have to accept the things in life we cannot change–as difficult as they may be. Some things are meant to be for a reason he said, and only God knows that reason. We had taken these children our love and God's love through a "love gift." Along with prayer, we had done all we could do.

It is true we cannot always see clearly into the "mirror of life" and understand all that lay within. As mortals, we question why, even though we are told not to put a question mark where God has a period.

As the scripture chosen for this chapter tells us, one day **we will understand** that which is now hidden by the veil that dims our eyes and dulls our understanding. I know when I meet the Master, my first question to him will be, "Why, Lord, why?"

Even though I felt I could not stand to see such things again, **we would return** to bring a smile to these children, yet another year, and seek God's strength; not only for us, but for his "little angels."

Florence B. Kinney

Be Thankful For The Little Things

Be THANKFUL for the little things

that swiftly pass by on angel wings;

A smile, a tear, a laugh, a hug

a joyous sunbeam ray

A rainbow arch, that bids farewell

to a quiet rainy day.

Be THANKFUL for a quiet hour

in which the mind can rest

For an hour spent alone with God

is one spent at its best.

Be THANKFUL for the bird's sweet song

that soothes the ear all day long;

For the towering mountains, the valleys green,

for the rush of the oceans; for beauty unseen.

Be THANKFUL for problems,

however great or small

for without them, there would always be a wall

Between God and man's desperate need

for a loving Father to intercede.

Be THANKFUL for the quiet night

as Earth, in its slumber, rests in His light

Be THANKFUL for the whispered prayer

for the assurance of peace, that tells us He cares.

Be THANKFUL for a God of Love

who sends these gifts from above.

Ye, be THANKFUL for all the little things

that pass by, swiftly, on angel wings.

Written by

Florence B. Kinney

Chapter 14

Working Through Adversity

"I will lift my eyes to the hills from whence comes my help. My help comes from the Lord who made heaven and earth." **Psalm 121:1-2**

The year 2002 had arrived and normal routine was the rule of the day. We were both working our jobs; mine full time and Charles was part time. This would be our fourteenth year of ministry and we were looking forward to all the planning that is involved in serving **thousands** of children for the holiday.

In May of this year, Charles had an appointment for a physical. On the appointment day, I was sitting in the doctor's waiting room when the doctor came out looking for me. As he approached me, I noticed a very concerned look on his face. He told me he was concerned about the results of one of the physical tests. He said Charles needed to see a certain specialist, but his name would have to go on a waiting list. He said, "It may not be anything serious but we need to be sure."

Three months passed before he was seen by the specialist. Within minutes of testing we were informed that Charles had a very serious form of cancer – one that is often fatal. To say the least, our world turned upside down and inside out. We had joined millions of others in this world who, also, felt the sting of the word cancer. We were swallowed up in a world of appointments, tests, surgeries, prayers for healing and all else that is attached to the dreaded word. We had been so caught up in the children's world of adversity, it was hard to believe adversity had now knocked on our door.

In September Charles would have very invasive surgery with the surgeon believing they had caught it in time. The prognosis was very hopeful. However, something the surgeon didn't expect happened. Due to the invasive surgery Charles would be left with complications that required a second surgery. Within weeks of the original surgery, he underwent another one. Unfortunately, the problem could not be corrected; however, the cancer was gone, so our future looked a bit brighter.

Our thoughts turned to our ministry as this was now Fall and the leaves were turning color. How could we focus on the children when our focus was on medical appointments, sometimes several a week? This was truly a difficult time for us. We would need to lift our eyes upward beyond the hills to a higher divinity. We would need to draw upon our faith both in heart and soul. We found ourselves sandwiched in between a life threatening disease and the ministry we had been called to fourteen years earlier. We were totally overwhelmed, yet, we knew God was our refuge and hope. We also knew **when you receive a "calling" from Heaven, you do not walk away!** A "calling" is ordained and continues on until the Lord, himself, calls you away from it.

We would have to call upon "our elves" more than ever, and depend on them for much of the workload. There were agencies and children depending on us. Not doing the project, was not an option!

Activity began once again at Santa's Workshop. Charles, being very weak, could not lift any cartons. Instead he helped sort, wrap book sets and fill requests. He worked diligently at my side, determined to bring a smile to the less fortunate. Meanwhile, as the word spread about our adversity, the community opened their hearts and arms to us, donating many gifts and hours of time helping process.

One lady in the community whom we had never met felt so touched by our determination to fill our "calling" donated her collection of happy meal toys, all mint in wrapped, unopened packages. She donated twelve complete sets of Snow White and the Dwarfs sets. Along with that, she brought us three bags of new toys for children under three years of age. All totaled, there were two hundred sixty-two gifts for God's "little ones." This gracious lady said **she felt led** to donate her collection that she had so enjoyed.

The Lord was at work; His Spirit moving over the community, bringing additional "elves" to our side. Churches offered their assistance in both donation of gifts and in helping process. Even some local organizations had our back. This all helped to raise our spirits, as Charles and I lived in a world of medical appointments, medical procedures and medical opinions.

Around this time, a young lady in a neighboring county, who was a Girl Scout Cadet earning her Silver Award, touched our hearts deeply. To earn her award it was necessary for her to complete thirty hours of community service. She chose Santa's Workshop for Hospitalized Children as her project. She would approach a large grocery chain asking them to help her in collecting new toys, stuffed animals and games for ill and needy children in our area. This young lady became dedicated to our cause and touched the hearts of many, including other children. Because of her example other little children wanted to take part. Other Girl Scouts came in to help. Even a dear friend's granddaughter helped wrap activity sets on the floor in her grandparent's home. We were being blessed in our time of adversity, but so were others. Lives were being touched all over the community, and were brought together in a common cause.

How wonderful to know our community had our back! From small children to senior citizens, the Workshop filled with sounds of laughter, and singing was accompanied by the merry ringing of the doorbell. We were going to make merry the hearts of many despite all that was consuming our main focus.

At this time, our church family came caroling! They first sang beautiful Christmas carols on our front porch looking in at the huge array of "love gifts" awaiting the children. Then they came inside, gathered around the gifts, and we all sang praises to an infant babe born two thousand years ago, who now, as the King of Kings had carried us through a difficult time.

Delivery time arrived. We would need added help since Charles could not lift. Neighbors offered assistance. One neighbor, who has offered the use of both of their vehicles for several years, was there for us once again. We also had the use of a van-on-loan, so there were plenty of "sleighs" to fill and plenty of folks to fill them.

We had been blessed indeed by the kindness and generosity of others. How happy we were to deliver to 1,650 ill and needy children in three locations. This would bring our total up to 27,000 youngsters since 1989, the year of our "calling."

Charles continued to get stronger and no further trace of cancer was found. We hung on to prayer each day and to hope for a full recovery.

I will always remember that beautiful Christmas Eve. We had just attended a lovely service, and as we left the service, I looked up to the Heavens. It was a beautiful holy night! As I began driving away from the little country church, Charles looked over at me and said, "Hon, I'm feeling better all the time. I think I'm going to make it."

I looked over at him and said, "I'm so glad you feel better. The greatest Christmas present I could receive this night would be that you will be completely well again."

As I close this chapter, I will share with you the experience I had right before a large delivery of gifts went to one of the hospitals. I chose to save this experience for last.

I was sitting on one of the stair steps which lead down from the upstairs hallway into our living room. Hundreds of little smiling faces looked up at me as I drank in the beautiful scene before me. The hours of hard work, the weariness of mind and body, and the distraction of focus due to illness all passed through my mind. I kept staring at all the "gifts of love" put together by loving, caring people, now ready to leave Santa's Workshop in the morning.

As I began to meditate at a midnight hour, still gazing at the delightful scene before me, I lifted my thanks to an awesome God, who had brought us through an adverse year, filling our every need from his storehouse of supply.

109 ࠂ

I then asked Him how much longer we would be allowed to carry out His ministry here on earth. Down in the very center of my being, words tumbled forth. The answer was: "Until the angels say amen." I felt a distinct chill ripple through my being. Charles and I then said "goodnight" to another wonderful season of "caring and sharing," that we had been blessed to have shared together.

Chapter 15

Until the Angels Say Amen

"To everything there is a season, and a time to every purpose under the heaven: a time to be born, and a time to die; a time to plant, and a time to pluck up that which is planted; a time to weep, and a time to laugh; a time to mourn, and a time to dance." **Ecclesiastes 3:1, 2, 4**

The year 2003 opened with a shadow hovering over us. It was months of hope, prayers that were unending, medical appointments and differing medical opinions. Charles was feeling much stronger by now and as the new year arrived, he was looking much healthier. We were told there was no sign of cancer. We were beginning to put our life back together. Then at the end of March, he began to experience some problems. Upon the completion of tests, we were advised that the cancer had returned full blown within three months time. He would be scheduled for twenty-eight radiations, which severely took their toll on him. Our world fell apart one more time. Enlisting the prayers of many people, we fought on and then a ray of hope.

Upon the completion of the radiation treatments, the surgeon advised us that the cancer had been destroyed. Charles was told he would have more good days than bad. We held on to hope and our faith. Nine days later, in the month of July, on a light rainy morning, Charles received the call that his eternal home was ready. Mr. Claus would have to leave us. He had been a very dedicated man to "our calling" and would be sorely missed. Not only did I lose my help mate and spouse of thirty-five years, but the community lost Mr. Claus. The words come to mind from a year earlier; the angels had said, "Amen".

After the whirlwind of activity that is involved with this type of situation began to subside, I began receiving inquiries as to the future of this ministry. I will share with you, in part, my answer to our friends and "elves".

"After much prayer and thought, I have decided to continue *Santa's Workshop for Hospitalized Children. I realize it will be a very emotional time for me, but I feel God calling Charles from earth's vineyard to Heaven's vineyard, is not sufficient reason to not touch an ill and needy child's life with God's love and our love. Charles*

smiling face will be missing, but his spirit will be present. *His* passion *and* legacy *for less fortunate children* will continue through us, *as God allows.*"

Only weeks later in September, with a "heavy heart", the foundation for another season of sharing was laid. It would not be as large an event as other years due to lack of time to focus. "Elves" gathered around me as well as family and friends. We planned our strategy for another season and began shopping for the children. We **knew** God would tap the shoulders of many in the community, which he did. Donations of gifts began arriving and I knew we would be just fine.

We added a family chiropractic group to our list of tree sponsors. The nursery of little tots requested fifty angel tags, even though there were only thirty youngsters. Seniors kept their knitting needles busy and activity was everywhere.

The mental health center we had served for years now merged with another health center, which meant many more requests would come our way. We would also add a local cancer house for children with cancer and their families to our list of recipients. They would be delighted to receive new stuffed animals and dollies to place in the bedroom of each child. What a joy to watch a tiny cancer victim hug a puppy against his chest; his little face just beaming; a moment of pain forgotten. Through watery eyes, what a joy to see!

In December, I would be asked once again, to speak at a local Coffee House in the fellowship center of a local church. What a difficult decision to make, as a smiling face was going to be missing at a nearby table. I truly felt sad and alone, but then I sensed these words: "Take my hand, child; we will do this together!" That is exactly what we did: we did it together, and I believe to this day, there was someone else with me that night; the God who called us to our ministry, myself, and a loving, dedicated man, who wished the best for less fortunate children. He gave of what little he had and shared it with a stranger's child. It was a great night. Many hearts were touched; many tears flowed and the legacy of a kind, thoughtful man was remembered.

Then a miracle—what would this sad chapter be like without a miracle? It would remain sad, but God loves to send a rainbow after the rain. He would do it again this year. Joy would enter our lives and we would smile again!

Again, without any knowledge on my part, there was a lady living in Nevada, who had a friend, who knew of our ministry. This friend shared our story with the lady in Nevada. She was so touched by our story that **she felt led to donate several hundred** small wrapped toys, mint condition, unopened, that she had enjoyed as a collection. She made contact with me from Nevada, and offered to bring them cross country rather than encumbering the cost of shipping. I could not believe what I was hearing. This lady was so touched by our ministry and my loss, she said she didn't mind making the trip. A couple weeks later, she pulled into our driveway, her car filled to capacity. Carton after carton of toys lined one long wall of our garage. This lady had brought more than toys. She brought joy not only to the children, but also to me. She was loving, caring and offered hugs. She knew what it was like to go through tough times and was willing to travel thousands of miles to comfort someone else in adversity. She was truly "a rainbow after the rain." She proved what a difference one person can make in the life of another. She was willing to move out of her comfort zone and touch a life with compassion and love thousands of miles away. I will forever remember that gracious lady.

The end of the year was closing in. It was time to load the "sleighs." I missed my helper terribly, but I **focused on the joy** the children would know on Christmas day. I thought about the surprise, the laughter, the squeals of delight that would fill hospital corridors and Mr. Claus smiling down on all of us. We would deliver 1,320 "gifts of love" despite a difficult year. All gifts were given in memory of my husband.

As I reflect back on one of the most difficult years of my life, I see our Lord's footprints in the "sand of our lives." As Charles' time grew closer, he turned to a very inspirational thought. He believed it was true, that when we only see one pair of footprints in adversity, it means we are being carried in the arms of a Sovereign Being. This inspirational thought was a comfort to him. For me, it has been a "main stay" in my daily living. I know beyond a doubt I was carried by a loving Father during those difficult days, and Charles said he **felt carried!**

This chapter has been one of sorrow and joy. As I mentioned in an earlier chapter, our Lord sends sunlight through the darkest moments of life, but he doesn't stop there. He tops those moments off with a rainbow. These are "gifts of love" from a loving Father to His children **everywhere**.

In closing, I would like to share this thought with you, the reader. As you read this chapter, if you also are going through adversity, it is my deepest prayer and hope that you will reach out to our Creator, grasp tight His hand and allow Him to carry you through your trial. Then bask in the sunlight; hold fast His rainbow and enjoy His companionship forevermore.

Now I close with these words: "Good night, Mr. Claus; Mrs. Claus will see you in the morning, when the angels say 'Amen.'"

Chapter 16

Seedtime and Harvest

"For God is the one who provides seed for the farmer and then bread to eat. In the same way, he will provide and increase your resources and then produce a great harvest of generosity in you." **2 Corinthians 9:10**

Having emerged from a two year "valley walk," a new year now rose before me. I found myself in the midst of the grieving process. When one loses a spouse of many years, especially where a close bond existed, there is a part of you that is also lost. The togetherness and the sharing in all things is found missing. It seemed as though I was existing with half a heart. Then I realized that he had half of my heart with him, and he left half of his heart here with me. Together, that gave each of us a whole heart again. Life would go on until we were together again in a heavenly place. I knew Charles would want this ministry to move forward. I believed he would encourage me from afar. Yet, a feeling past through me that maybe he wasn't that far away; maybe his spirit was here right beside me. He would always be there for me, as the bond between us could not be broken. To this very day, he lives within my heart and he is never far away.

Thus the year 2004 began. I knew in my heart I would need to refocus if this ministry was to stay alive. I would need to see beyond the grief, just as in a preceding chapter of this book, a "man in white" showed us how to see beyond the gift in a package. It was time to plant "new seed."

The harvest was ripe; seeds of love, hope, compassion, faith and trust all needed planting. It became a **"time of renewal."** I knew a faithful God would walk beside me. He would help me accomplish every dream that he had placed in my heart. I also realized that if I continued to use the talents and gifts he had given Charles and me, he would provide the resources. Then he would gather in the harvest. Our Lord provides the seed and places it within us; we only have to **activate that seed**. He will grow that seed and **wonderful amazing things will happen; lives will be touched for Him!**

This year of 2004, we would be serving three hospitals, the merged Mental Health Centers, our local cancer house and a community center for the needy. A busy season was ahead!

Wish lists and urgently needed lists soon arrived as Fall made its call. We quickly realized the increase in requests. I knew I would need even more "community elves" to help Mrs. Claus.

Then, **totally unexpectedly**, several automotive agencies in our area began to respond to our ministry. They decided to take part in collecting new toys, games and stuffed animals. What a blessing this proved to be! They would place a little tagged tree in their showroom or office area asking employees and their customers if they would like to remember an ill and needy child for the holiday. The amazing result was 2,445 new gifts just from the automotive world! What a blessing for us from a faithful God! Many new "community elves" took part in gladdening the heart of a less fortunate child.

As the weeks passed by, I began hearing of children who were not going to have a Santa visit in their homes. These were outpatient children whose parents were financially depleted by medical bills. This is always very disturbing and it pulls at my heart string. I was determined to meet this challenge head on. We were being "blessed" with additional resources at the Workshop. These "seeds of love" were meant to be planted in the lives of thousands of the Lord's "little ones." Every child and family that were reported to Santa's Workshop would have a Santa visit, again kept anonymous.

I would like to share a story as related to me. In one of these homes, a mother of a two year old and a five year old had absolutely no funds available for Christmas giving. Her hope was for a small tree with a few lights. At least the children would have something to look at for the holiday. The sad part was there would be no presents under the small tree for anyone. How do you tell a child, who already shows a wonderment in its eyes for such a magical time of year, that Santa can't make it this year? You try to express to that child that it has nothing to do with being naughty or nice, as some children relate to this expression often heard at Christmas, and feel they are at fault. You try to assure them Santa has problems at times, just like all of us. Hopefully, he will be able to visit them next year. Can you imagine the sadness in the heart of a child? Think back to the excitement we felt as a child; that should give us an answer.

Returning to the story of this young mother, Santa's Workshop, of course, donated several lovely gifts to be placed under the tree. This mother didn't wish for anything for herself; just for "the kids." Later that mother shared her story with hospital personnel: *Around 3 a.m. on Christmas morning, she awoke to voices in the downstairs. Tiptoeing to the head of the stairs she viewed two little curly heads. There, sitting on the floor facing the small tree, with little legs crossed, were her two little ones. She heard one child say to the other, "What do you think Santa brought us?" They were deep into a world of wonderment at three o'clock in the morning. Little did they realize that Santa had brought them "seeds of love", "hope" and "compassion." Hopefully, those seeds were planted in the lives of those children, and one day they would plant their seeds in another life here on earth. The mother wept for the kindness of someone she would never meet.*

She was amazed, also, that as small as her children were in age, neither one touched or opened anything. They waited patiently for Mom to join them later. Mother would also find a little package for herself on Christmas morning. After all, Santa double checks his list before he loads his sleigh.

One day when these children become adults will they, too, plant seeds in some else's life? **Only God above knows and sees the impact!** He, alone, gathers in the harvest. A harvest that would not be there without the sowing of the seed. We as his children are called to be his "seed planters." The Lord will handle the seed process himself. Not one of us can say there is nothing we can do and be truthful. There is just no such thing. There will always be need in the world and always a need for responders. My prayer and hope for you, the reader, as you read this chapter, is this: that your heart will be touched and you will become a "responder" to the needs of another human being.

I mentioned earlier in this chapter I needed to refocus and **see beyond the gift** and the **impact** it makes on an ill or needy child's life.

According to hospital personnel, here are some of the benefits a child receives through our "seed gift." First, a gift provides diversion from their suffering and helps them to relax. Secondly, the child feels more secure in a strange environment. Third, a Santa gift helps to lessen stress of separation and feelings of home sickness. Fourth, a gift also provides a means for release of tension and expression of feelings. Last, a surprise gift provides the means for accomplishing therapeutic goals when using play for procedures. These benefits are the wonderful results of the giving. They make a huge difference in the life of that child.

Recently, I had the pleasure of speaking with a young adult, who advised me of a time when she was a small child and had to be hospitalized. What does she remember up front? A teddy bear that laid on her bed the day of her arrival. Amazingly she still has that bear! It reminds her of a "moment of joy" she experienced in a scary environment. I was thrilled to hear her story and thanked her for sharing it with me. A "seed" of love and caring was planted in her young life and she would forever remember. I pray she is sharing seeds with others in her everyday life.

As the year was coming to a close, many needs were being met by community once again. The "new elves" from the automotive field made a huge difference in needs being met. Adding these "elves" to our regular giving "elves" from all corners of the community would bring us another wonderful season of sharing. All totaled 3,587 "gifts of love", all seed provided by an awesome Heavenly Father, planted into the lives of His children by his responders.

I ask this question—do we have the fertile soil within our hearts that is required for seeds to flourish? If we do not, do we wish to have it? All it requires is to reach out, ask our Lord to place those seeds in our heart along with the fertile soil. Then let him do the watering of our hearts garden and enjoy the flowers bloom.

It now seemed as though my life was moving forward as, once again, I felt the joy of giving. Then another difficult blow—my Mom, who had been a "charter elf," who loved our ministry and became an integral part of it, began failing rapidly with her health. Right before delivery time, she asked me to bring her three book sets to wrap. She had **wrapped thousands of** these sets over the course of fifteen years.

She wanted so badly to wrap a few more. I took three sets to her. Because she was so weak from ebbing strength, it proved difficult for her to accomplish the task, but she was determined.

I watched her wrap for the last time, with a smile on her face; yet hurt in her heart. She did not want to leave her family, but said she had to go. It was her time – one week before Christmas, just as we began deliveries to make glad the hearts of children, God called Mom to her eternal home. A beautiful lady, who loved God and her family would be another smiling face so missed at Santa's Workshop. The most loving and caring mother a child could ever know had brightened THOUSANDS of stranger's children's lives, always "humming a tune" as she wrapped sets and filled cartons with baby items placed just a certain way, her hands touching them with her love.

Was I prepared for another loss? Certainly not! Would I need to draw even deeper into my faith? I certainly would. I kept thinking back to a mother, who was so strong in her beliefs and shared that strength with her children. She taught us "the golden rule" early in life and set us the example of giving. She lived a life of others first, she last. I learned from that and was determined to be just like her. We shared our name, our faith, our goals in life, right down to love of flowers. She would always be "the flower of my life." She would be sorely missed by her family, friends and the "elves" of Santa's Workshop.

Another valley would be mine to walk through for a while, but as I rested my grief in the arms of the Lord, I heard the words "be strong." I have heard those same words many times since.

As this joyful and sad month of December 2004 was drawing to a close, news reports began telling of a tragedy of tragedies in a far off country called India. A tsunami would sweep over parts of the nation and cause immense suffering and loss. Would Santa's Workshop be a responder?

Plant Your Seeds

My Friend, have you planted any "seeds" today?
Have you comforted the lonely,
or have you turned away?
On your journey, did you see
the hungry and the lost?
Did you share with them, your abundance, or
did you figure it would be too great a cost?

And those you passed, who knew great sorrow
Did you offer words of comfort, or did you
figure it could wait until tomorrow?

And the helpless victims of man's earthly greed
Did you offer words of faith, upon
which their Souls could feed?
And to the one so downcast, who
desperately needed a friend,
Did you offer your friendship, or
did you turn away again?
My Friend, again, I ask you
Have you planted any "seeds" today?
Have you brightened another life
As you journey along life's way?

Have you taken time for others
Or have you failed to see
What Ye have done unto these, my Brethren
Ye have done it unto me.

Written by
Florence B. Kinney

Chapter 17

Comfort One Another

*"Blessed be the God and Father of our Lord, Jesus Christ, the Father of mercies and **God of all Comfort, who comforts us** in all our tribulation, that we may be able **to comfort those who are in any trouble**, with the comfort with which we ourselves are Comforted by God." **2 Corinthians 1:3, 4***

The year 2005 would begin with one of the deadliest natural disasters in recorded history. Thousands of miles from America's shores, in a country called India, in a body of water called the Indian Ocean, an undersea mega thrust earthquake would devastate part of this land. Hundreds of thousands of innocent lives would be swallowed up in tidal waves racing onto shore. Many small fishing villages were horrifically hit and very little humanity remained. Little children, men and women could not withstand the surging waters and were washed away. Those who were spared watched parents and siblings float away amid turbulent, angry waters.

Years earlier, a man from India and a woman from America met at a college in the United States and later married.

The man felt a "calling" to return to India. Upon his return, he was "called" to found a co-educational Christian Bible College, where many who would receive an education would also be introduced to Christianity.

Then the tsunami hit with all its fury. Many little children were left orphans roaming the streets looking for food and shelter. The man who initiated the College contacted his wife here in America. He advised her something needed to be done about the dazed, lost little souls.

He now felt a "deeper calling" to establish a home for these children. In addition to establishing the Bible College, he expanded his mission to include an orphanage built within an oasis of beautiful flowers and trees, creating a home and school surrounded by beauty. Here these displaced "little ones" would be provided an education and security until they reached adulthood and could be on their own. Many were introduced to Christianity for the first time.

The owners of this orphanage felt the children lacked something small to call their own. They were left with no possessions, not even a toy. Something small and cuddly to comfort them would be even better, but what?

About this time, this man's wife made contact with our little country church. This orphanage had touched the hearts of our parishioners and had become a part of our mission work. She mentioned the children had no personal possessions; nothing to hold or hug. It was determined that a beanie baby would be ideal for a child to love. They would have a "little friend" to comfort them and call their own. It was determined they could use two hundred new beanie babies.

While all these things were transpiring in a far off land, back in the states, called America, a lady was sitting in her vehicle at an intersection waiting for the traffic light to turn green. You might even call it a fork in the road. That lady was me. As I was waiting for the light to change, in the quiet, words rose within me. These words were: *"You are to take one hundred dollars to your brother for beanie babies."* I was told which brother, since I have three of them. At first, I was a bit confused as to what I was hearing, but then the words were repeated. I knew something was about to happen. The Lord had a plan that we would need to follow. On Friday of that very week, upon receiving my weekly paycheck, I removed one hundred dollars and took it immediately to my brother.

Talk about a "leap of faith!" I explained, in the best way I could, that I had been told to give him this money and for him to search out new beanie babies for little orphans in India. Needless to say, he was stunned and puzzled.

He asked me, "Where am I supposed to find these beanie babies and why me?"

I replied, "I do not know, but God does."

I told him we had need of two hundred and hopefully within a two week period of time. My brother accepted a one hundred dollar bill from me and sort of grinned. I advised him this was for real. Now at this particular time, new Ty beanie babies were selling at five dollars apiece. We needed at least two hundred and only had one hundred dollars. That meant we could only pay fifty cents apiece. It seemed most unlikely that anyone would sell us new beanie babies for fifty cents each. It seemed to us impossible, but we remembered **"all things are possible with God."**

A week passed by, and then a phone call from my brother. He asked me to come to his office. He had something to show me. When I arrived, there before my unbelieving eyes, were cartons and bags of **new Ty beanie babies** greeting me. My first question was, "Where did you find them?"

He related this miraculous story:

As he was about to close his office for the day, a customer, as he was leaving, asked my brother if he was going to a community garage sale of forty or more homes that was an annual event in a neighboring development. My brother advised he had no plans to attend. Then he related to me **he felt led** to go.

After having walked home to home for several hours looking for beanie babies, there was one last home sitting upon a knoll. There was a steep incline leading up to this home, one that seemed nearly impossible for him to walk due to extreme fatigue from a painful back condition. He was about to turn away, when again, he **felt a certainty** that he was to make the incline to this home.

As he approached the garage entry way, there before him were cartons and bags of **new** beanie babies–just what we needed for the little orphans. My brother inquired if they all were for sale. Receiving an affirmative, he explained he could only give her fifty cents apiece.

He explained where they were needed and about the dire circumstances of the little ones in India. The lady advised him there were over a hundred plus beanie babies there. She was not sure of the exact number.

He said, "I need all of them; would you accept just one hundred dollars for them? That is all I can offer you."

The lady's heart was touched as she said, "Help me gather them up."

I ask you, the reader, was there divine intervention that day? Was there a "Divine Being" making it all happen?

From the moment I heard the words of direction within me, the obedience to follow that direction, my brother open to the need, the customer who would tell him of the community sale, and the lady whose heart was touched with compassion, all were part of the Master's plan *for His little orphans thousands of miles from America's shores.*

Through His Divine Spirit, a couple from India, a lady in America **open to His calling** and parishioners from a little country church, brought much needed comfort to His little ones across the waters. With a **handful left over,** Santa's Workshop donated, with joy, one hundred sixty five new Ty beanie babies and the little country church shared thirty-five. All totaled, two hundred "gifts of love" for little souls who needed to be loved.

Truly, **another wonderful miracle** from a **miracle planning God**; a miracle that touched two different countries.

A postscript to this story ~

One anniversary year later of this tragic event, a lady from the little country church would visit this orphanage on their first Christmas, as a mission trip. The purpose of this trip was to bring hope, compassion and comfort.

What would greet her? Beanie babies displayed at the entryway and these cuddly little animals inside still bringing comfort and a smile to each child. This lady was asked to speak to the children. They expressed their sadness and loss by drawing pictures of family floating away in angry, mucky waters before their eyes. Would they ever be able to forget such tragedy? I'm sure not, but would they find hope again? Yes, with the help of an awesome, universal, yet personal "Divine Being" and those He would choose to take their hand, walk with them down life's journey, and love them eternally, they would have a new beginning.

Yes, we are **to comfort** those in trial, just as the **Lord comforts us** in our tribulations. What comfort a small beanie baby can bring to a child who has nothing. Were those small cuddly animals a conduit of God's love from us to them? Most definitely and **they will remember**.

Santa's Workshop 2005 would prove to be one of the most eventful years to date. This would be the first year we would receive so many beautiful bunnies, we would be able to surprise ill children in the hospitals and cancer house at Easter. The rainbow colors of these adorable creatures delighted the eye and soul of these children.

As the nation across the waters began their healing process in working through their adversity, another horrific natural disaster would strike back here on our shores. It was September 2005 and a time of utter devastation for parts of our country. As the end days of August approached, a deadly hurricane formed over the Bahamas, strengthening in the Gulf of Mexico, making land fall in southeast Louisiana. The city of New Orleans would flood due to failure of the levee system. Severe flooding would cause hundreds of thousands of displaced residents along the Gulf Coast, home after home completely destroyed. The coast line of Mississippi would also be ravaged by flooding. This hurricane called Katrina, would be classified as one of the worst natural disasters in United States history.

Many displaced people were sent to San Antonio, Texas, for shelter. Shelters were set up at an air force base providing not only a roof for shelter, but food and medicinal care also. As I watched the heart wrenching pictures filling the television screen, I felt the Lord's Spirit move within me, once again. The little children left with nothing were here in our own land. They had joined the cries of other stricken children in the world. I knew I had to do something, even if it was small. Even small beats nothing at all!

About this time, the same lady, from the little country church, mentioned earlier, received her "calling" to once again go forth and witness to hurting humanity.

She would go to San Antonio to help serve at different shelters. The Lord called me, once again, to bring comfort and compassion to His "little ones" in those shelters. I would carton and bag two hundred ten new small stuffed animals along with new beanie babies to send to the affected children. Santa's Workshop was again called to action to serve a hurting humanity.

Where there was nothing, there would be something! It is better to give even a little, than nothing at all.

There was no way I could gift hundreds of thousands of displaced children, but Santa's Workshop **could make a**

difference in the lives of a couple hundred. Again, joy filled my heart; yet mixed with sadness, as I so wished I could have done more. The other avenue open to me was prayer. That avenue was used daily.

Outside of adult collections, beanie babies are normally associated with children. However, while the lady from the little country church was ministering at the shelter, an ill man living in the shelter dormitory would come to the medical clinic each day. Each day he refused to enter the clinic to receive the medicine he needed. One day, this lady saw him standing outside, looking into the clinic. She went out to greet him and sat down beside him. She began asking him a few questions. This lady then learned he had a very ill wife in one of the shelter dormitories. He was concerned for her and wished to give her a present to express his love for her.

He mentioned he had seen some small stuffed animals of different kinds and wondered if he could select one for her. He, of course, was referring to the beanie babies sent from Santa's Workshop. As he selected one, a smile covered his face. He did this "act of caring" before he would accept any medicine for himself.

A few days later, the lady from church visited the dormitory where a very ill lady sat on a cot. There on a pillow where her head would rest lie the beanie baby - **a comfort in the midst of turmoil and helplessness.**

Comfort one another is not just a wish of God's heart but a rule we are to follow in our everyday living. When we comfort our neighbor, not only here, but around the world, we shall be truly comforted by the God of all comfort.

In November, Santa's Workshop would be remembered by the community at the annual choir festival; a beautiful, inspirational program that draws a huge crowd each year. The sponsor of this program has been part of our "elf family" for many years. They have made a difference in the success of this ministry.

In early December, Mrs. Claus would be surprised and awe struck by the community of businesses, entertainers, and good friends who agreed to participate in a fundraiser to help me continue the ministry after having suffered great loss in the deaths of Charles and "elf Mom". They would sponsor a Christmas in the Village program, along with other events. The evening of the event, heavy wet snow began covering the streets and driving was a concern. Yet, folks came out in holiday spirit and the snowy night seemed to add to the wonderful event. Amid music, refreshments, speeches and holiday merriment, many ill and needy children in our area would have a Christmas. The "communion of community" was at its peak that special evening, and fun was had by all.

Santa's Workshop for Hospitalized Children would never forget all the different pathways the Lord had placed before us. The road stretched long this particular year – from orphans in India to hurricane victims in Louisiana and Texas; then on to local hospitals, a cancer center, needy community centers, mental health centers and yes, even several hundred needy youngsters who were not going to have a Christmas at all. We would also add another local community center to our list which services the needy.

All totaled, 3,587 "gifts of comfort" would be distributed, all given in memory of my Mom. As the year 2005 came to a close, the mighty hand of God moved over everything. An awesome divine being smiled down on a lady and her "elves" serving His children around the world, and blessed us everyone with His comfort and His love.

Day By Day

Day by day, Dear Lord, I pray

For guidance and wisdom, at work and at play

For light sufficient that my eyes may see

Your love in all of humanity.

Day by day, Dear Lord, I ask

For grace sufficient to meet each task

For your powerful presence to dwell within me

That I may be a "beacon" for others to see.

Day by day, Dear Lord, I pray

That your love be with me more each day

Keep me in humility; lead me in the way

For this I pray, Dear Lord, day by day.

Written by

Florence B. Kinney

Chapter 18

Prayer and Miracles

Ask, and it shall be given you; seek and ye shall find;
knock and it shall be opened unto you; for everyone
that asketh receiveth; and he that seeketh findeth; and
to him that knocketh it shall open. **Matthew 7:7,8**

Over the past twenty-three years of this "Christ-Called" ministry, we have received answer to prayer over and over again. A number of times, answered prayer has been followed with a "rainbow of miracles".

In earlier chapters of this book I have shared with you some of these miracles. In the following chapters, you will read of awesome moments when miracles crossed our pathways once again and touched the lives of families, elves and children.

This particular year of 2006 would open with a wonderful surprise. In fact, I named it a "God-wink." We found it necessary to raise our budget to a higher cost level. Costs were rising steadily and we now had to figure on five to eight dollars an item.

Then another wonderful phone call in February. A lady who operated a card and gift shop in our area called to advise me she was going out of business. She had extra stock available; cute white puppies with red hats holding an adorable red heart in between their paws. These were expensive stuffed animals that normally we would not have been able to afford. She wondered if we could use them at Santa's Workshop. Of course, my answer was in the affirmative. She advised I could purchase them at half price. I was elated as this was good news for our struggling budget. Through the kindness of this lady, many hospitalized children and cancer patients had a Valentine surprise. One more God directed phone call had made a difference in the lives of His children.

As Easter approached, beautiful multi-colored soft cuddly bunnies began to arrive. These were totally unexpected and so welcome! A family member had found a stuffed animal outlet and purchased over one hundred of them enabling us to bless His little people with their own Easter bunny. What a blessing these two events proved to be! We were blessed to receive these items, and the children were blessed through our giving. Both events were unexpected and morale was high at the Workshop. We saw these events as "God winks." They made everyone smile.

This year we would introduce newborns up to one year olds with precious little sock dollies. The hospitals loved them along with baby rattles. We were able to purchase them at a certain store which went out of business. We could no longer find them as time went on. Then ladies in the little country church decided they would make them. Each year hereafter the most precious little sock dollies in rainbow colors have arrived at the hospital nurseries warming the hearts of all who see them. They are stuffed with love, stitched with love, and given in love.

This particular Fall we received urgent requests for basketballs for the "cottage children" so they could interact with each other, enjoying the outdoors. This Mental Rehabilitation Center was home away from home for many displaced children. The cost of these balls was above our budgeted amount. As I visited store after store, I found no relief on the high pricing. One day I was standing in the sports aisle looking at these basketballs. I began to pray, telling God we could not afford them and they were so needed for His troubled children. Then I remember telling Him it would be OK if we had to skip them this particular year, as we had other items for them. It was just a wish of my heart to fill their requests.

Two nights later, as we were having dinner, the doorbell rang. As I opened the door, my eyes beheld several huge bags containing twenty-five new basketballs. A neighboring family **felt led** to purchase them as a surprise. The gentleman looked at me standing in amazement, and said, "I hope you can use these." I began to weep, as I realized someone in another realm of existence had heard this lady's prayer in a store aisle and decided to answer her prayer with a miracle.

Perhaps you may wonder how such a miracle could come to pass. I don't have all the answers, but I would like to share with you a few thoughts about prayer and miracles as they have related to my life. Prayer is a direct channel between God and His children. Prayer and miracles are companions in life. One seems to be necessary in order to receive the other. In life there are prayers we offer to God that do not require miracles. Then there are prayers we offer up to Him in which we ask for a miracle. There also are prayers offered where hope rests in the center of one's heart; yet we fail to directly ask. The scripture for this chapter tells us to ask, seek and knock.

When our prayer is **filled with love** for God and His children everywhere, it becomes a "power prayer." It rises up to the very throne of God and is heard.

Next our belief system takes over; hope rises within us and expectation causes the result. We **believe**, we **hope**, we **expect** a Sovereign being to meet our need and He does. A sincere prayer avails much; a few sincere words from our heart touches the heart of God. I also found that **seeking His will** for our lives and **following his direction and guidance** makes all the difference. Do miracles always follow prayer? Certainly not, but many times and at unexpected times, they do follow a loving, sincere prayer. We are told in scripture that God looks upon the heart.

I see miracles as rainbows in life that are sent to lift our spirit, to reinforce our belief system, to lift us up on eagle's wings, so we may witness to His power and majesty to everyone. A world without miracles would be a dull place indeed. It is up to each of us to **be open to His miracles. They hover above us, move around us, and bless us** more than we would ever realize. We need to open our eyes to the miracle of each day, and to the God of miracles who sends them to earth.

This year of 2006 would close once again with overflowing gurneys, loaded sleighs, stacked cartons of new clothing and many joyous smiles. We would close this year with a total of 37,306 "gifts of love" since our "calling" in 1989. What an incredible journey; yet more lay ahead.

Chapter 19

Divine Appointments

Peace I leave with you, my peace I give to you; not as the world gives do I give to you. Let not your heart be troubled, neither let it be afraid. **John 14:27**

"Move a little closer", I heard the nurse say. It was December 2007. I had just completed a tour of the children's ward along with various other departments. Mrs. Claus was delivering stuffed animals known as "specials" and dollies for hospitalized little folk at Christmas.

The nurse manager had just advised me there was one more patient to visit if I were willing. This time it was not an ill child, but a dying eighty-nine year old lady. This would be the first time I had been asked to visit a dying adult patient.

As I moved further into the darkened room and close to her bed, I was told to hold the large teddy bear up by her face, where oxygen fed into her nostrils helping her to breathe. She had definitely begun her journey home. I was advised this lady had always loved large teddy bears. Did I have any left over from my tour of the wards? I did not think so, but returning to the nurse's station there lay one remaining lovely light colored large teddy bear in a plastic bag. There was no doubt in my mind that teddy bear had been meant for her.

As the nurses turned her face toward me, they said, "Look, look what this lady brought you!" Her eye lids suddenly began to quiver; then her eyes opened for a moment, a **joy filled** sound of "ah-ooo" was heard and then her eyes closed.

A short time later, she would see through "spiritual eyes" her new home and the Lord who placed me at her bedside at the right hour; His timing to be perfect. A divine appointment to be sure and a memory forever embedded within me.

This year of 2007 I was asked to visit several children right before Christmas, surprising them with a visit of holiday cheer and a "Santa" gift. Normally this was something Charles and I declined, as we felt our place was "in the wings" **providing the joy and excitement of the holiday**; not out front with personal visits.

However, as the years passed, I finally agreed to make a few personal visits each Christmas. At times it proved to be emotionally draining, yet very rewarding. Just to see the surprised grin and the smile of delight makes everything worthwhile.

One little girl was surprised with a white teddy bear. As I handed her the bear, her eyes met mine as she said, "You have made me happy!" Another toddler was exhausted from crying and had fallen asleep. His Mom lay alongside him in the bed near his crib. Not wishing to awaken him, I gave her an adorable puppy to surprise her little son. She then laid the puppy near her son's head, resting it high upon the pillow. What a touching moment as she said, "When my son wakes up he will be surprised by a new friend. It will mean everything to him, as it does to me."

Another divine appointment? I have come to believe each visit that I have made over the years of this ministry have truly been divine appointments.

In another room a young girl was being taken for testing. As I spoke to her on the gurney she noticed the dressed up teddy bear in my arms. I assured her the bear would be waiting for her upon her return. As she was wheeled down the hallway I entered her room, gently placed the bear in the center of her bed, its head resting on her pillow. I spoke from my heart to this stuffed animal resting before me, "Bring her comfort little bear, bring her comfort." Upon her return, she too, would hold a new friend in her arms. Another moment of happiness and comfort would be recorded in my mind and also in another realm, for even God would have to smile!

In emergency I met a little boy around three years old. He was sobbing uncontrollably, tears not only wet against his little cheeks but falling onto his clothing as well. I tried to comfort him with an adorable puppy. He just looked away and continued to sob. After several tries, his mother approached me.

She said, "May I accept the puppy on behalf of my son? You see, **he hurts much too much right now**. When he is better he will love his new puppy."

As I gave her the puppy I felt my heart would rip out of my chest. The inner pain I felt for this child was incredible. I met him sobbing and I left him sobbing. No one and nothing could seem to stop the continuous flow of tears. To see a child hurting that badly tore at my very being.

Another story I would like to share with you, the reader, remains strong in my memory. An adorable little girl in the outpatient department was drawn to my attention. She and her mom were trying to find a way home. Since the mother did not have available funds for even a bus she was calling number after number seeking a ride. I was advised there was a very bleak outlook for any Christmas festivities in her home. She and her family would not have much of a holiday. "Would you have a little something for her?" I was asked.

Indeed, I had a delightful new rag doll with blonde hair, a yellow top, orange slacks and little red sandals on its feet. It was so colorful and cheery. Walking toward this little girl with this rag doll in my hands, it seemed like her eyes had doubled in size. A grin spread from ear to ear. I asked her if she would like a new friend to play with. She looked up at me with sparkling eyes and said, "Oh, yes, thank you." She looked about four years old. Her mom stood nearby looking very sad and tired. As I began to walk away, I heard a loud voice call out, "Wait!" I turned around to see a sobbing mother who was pointing a finger toward me. She cried out, "God bless you!"

My tears joined hers. Here was a distraught mother who was so appreciative a stranger would take the time to seek out her child for a "moment of joy", place a hand upon her child's little shoulder, and wish her a Merry Christmas. Someone cared and a difference was made for that hurting family. Divine appointment? I will let you decide.

These visits bring joy to a hurting and often frightened child. The warm inner glow I receive from these "special holy moments" remain with me daily. One does not forget something so special.

There are thousands of children right here in America who would love a visit from someone who cares about them. Could it be you? Would you be willing to set some time aside for a hurting child? I pray these questions will rest upon your heart. These little children need us! They need to know they are loved, even if it is a stranger's love. They need to find a peace in the circumstance they are in; a peace that comes from above and allows us to be the conduit of that peace. The scripture for this chapter states "Let not your heart be troubled, neither let it be afraid." **It is our responsibility to reach out to these troubled hearts and calm their fears.**

If you would like to enrich the lives of others and have your life enriched in return, begin a ministry of your own. You will be taken to places you have never been!

As this year drew to a close I was thrilled to add a local insurance agency to our list of participants. These "elves" decided to purchase a gift for a child in need in place of giving a gift to each other. They have remained "elves" right up to this current writing. These folks have brought joy to many ill and needy youngsters.

Also joining us would be a musical group of folks who donate their time, talent and funds to charitable causes. We are grateful for everyone's participation.

This year of 2007 would close with the distribution of 1,416 "Santa" gifts bringing many smiles to the faces of His little ones and a peace to little troubled hearts. For just a little while they forgot their fears and smiled.

Chapter 20

His Lamp and His Light

Your word is a lamp to guide my feet and a light for my path. **Psalm 119:105**

The Fall of 2008 at Santa's Workshop for Hospitalized Children would become one of the busiest seasons ever. I had no idea another focus would be ours. This time new warm clothing would be urgently needed and requested. It was brought to my attention we had **six thousand needy children** in our area who would face a harsh winter without proper clothing. These little heads, hands and feet needed to be clothed.

It was pointed out to me the need was so great it had to be dealt with on a larger scale. Would I be willing to birth a community clothing drive? My first thought was could I possibly handle this task along with the workshop activities. Within a few moments of praying the answer was clear. The Lord was "calling" me a second time. We would need to move **further out of our comfort zone** and reach His "little ones" with basic necessities.

Once more a lantern was lit within my being. I knew the Lord would light my pathway showing me where to go and what to do. I would pray for guidance and strength to do His will, as this would require many additional hours of work. In fact, many more days and nights would be encumbered, and I was still working full time.

Thus, in November, the "Only One" Community Clothing Drive was born. It seemed ironic that nineteen years ago, Charles and I had started our ministry with two little toy trucks. Now it would be one pair of mittens, one neck scarf, one hat and one pair of socks. Yes, we had little children with no socks in their shoes. We had children facing the cold with bare heads and bare hands.

I remember the Sunday afternoon I **was led** to drawing up a flyer telling of the urgent need in the surrounding community. I ran one hundred copies, distributing them home to home in my development. That was the beginning. I then enlisted the help of a couple local newspapers who ran articles on the need I expressed. I realized people would need drop off and collection locations. I contacted a few businesses asking if we could place a collection box in their foyer or office area. The response was in the affirmative. These locations were advertised and we were on our way. Over the course of the next few weeks, the community's response was awesome. Beautiful knitted hats, scarves and mittens along with store purchased items began filling collection boxes. Hundreds of pairs of new socks ranging from new born to teenager were donated. The lantern that had been lit within me was now being lit in the hearts of hundreds of people. **God's light shone with a radiance** over all participating. Folks who had been knitting hats, scarves and mittens during the year and did not know who the recipient would be, now knew! Parents and their children visited stores purchasing warm pieces of clothing for those they did not know. It was truly miraculous seeing everyone coming together for a wonderful cause. God's "storehouse of supply" opened and a true miracle was witnessed, as 2,100 new articles of clothing filled the family room of my home. Every color of the rainbow was present as moist eyes surveyed the scene before them. It caused the "elves" and me to reflect upon the scriptural story of the "loaves and fishes."

We started with one article of clothing and ended with 2,100 articles of clothing. It taught me that **our Lord's**

provision is always there! We only need to seek His guidance and complete His will for our lives.

As the weeks passed, the hum of elf activity increased. This would be the year of the Dalmatian at Santa's Workshop. I would find a great deal on adorable Dalmatian puppies, enabling us to donate over fifty of these little creatures. We would have the same good fortune in finding rag dollies. These are always such a delight to a little girl. I have watched little girls hold them close to their heart, tucking them in for the night in their hospital room. What a precious moment to behold! One little girl hugged her new friend. Looking at me, she said, "I love my new dolly." This meant the world to me. It makes everything fall into perspective and warms the soul of the giver and receiver.

We realized we would need the Lord to tap more shoulders and touch more hearts as collecting, counting, sorting, wrapping, packaging increased and hours lengthened. What a joy to see busy "elves" filling each room of the workshop with merriment and holiday spirit! As information reached our distribution locations, the numbered requests for new clothing poured in. Those requests would top our usual top ten request list. I could see the Lord leading us into another dimension of ministry. It was wonderful!

As more and more stories came our way of children in need of **simple necessities**, that we, who are fortunate take for granted, my heart swelled with joy as carton after carton were stacked higher and higher in the rooms. Those abundantly filled cartons were "blessings" going out to "bless" others. Not only would heads, hands and feet be warmed through a cold season, but little hearts as well.

This year of 2008 would close with much joy in many hearts. Tears of happiness and thankfulness moistened the cheeks of many staff members, as loaded "sleighs" delivered 2,933 toys, games, stuffed animals, activity sets and new articles of warm clothing. It would be a very "snowy" number of deliveries, which made them all the more miraculous.

It is said that each snowflake that falls to earth is different. They are each "specially designed" by our Creator. Likewise, these "little ones" we serve here on earth are a "special design" from the same Creator of the snowflakes. They require warmth, love and tender loving care. The scripture tells of Jesus laying his hands upon them and blessing them. We have the opportunity in life of doing the same. I am so humbled to have been "called" to this new dimension of ministry.

My deepest thanks to all who have joined me in this "God called" endeavor.

Chapter 21

Miracles and Angels

For He shall give His angels charge over thee, to keep thee in all thy ways. They shall bear thee up in their hands, lest thou dash thy foot upon a stone. **Psalm 91:11, 12**

A new year had dawned and what an exciting year it would be! However, before all the joy and excitement, we would experience sadness first. In March of this year of 2009, a "dedicated elf" of Santa's Workshop would be called to her eternal home. This lady loved our ministry to children and played an important role at the Workshop for many years. She loved to wrap book sets and fill cartons with a variety of gifts. She was a lovely, caring neighbor who shared her enthusiasm for our ministry with family and friends. She truly "advertised" our goal to bring comfort and joy to the less fortunate. She is sorely missed by all.

Months of planning and shopping for the children began. We no longer had the joy of serving many less fortunate children in one of the local hospitals, as it had closed earlier. Another hospital we had served for many years was now receiving only book sets. Their children were being serviced by another gentleman, mentioned earlier in this book, with his toy ministry. He is able to share toys all year long. Slowly, our time there became less. Today we supply stuffed animals to their cancer wing only. This brought us down to one remaining hospital, which we serve to this day. It is such a joy to still bring happiness to these ill children. We are so warmly received there and everyone is so appreciative of our endeavor.

This year we would continue to provide gifts for the Mental Health Centers, our local cancer house, and community centers serving the needy.

The months passed swiftly. Soon the first signs of Autumn appeared. A busy season lay ahead. It was at this point in time miraculous events began to happen. It was the morning of October 3, 2009. I was awakening from sleep when the following words rose up within me and were heard clearly through my being: *"Remember Jesus Christ is your sponsor and you are the chosen of the vineyard and all who participate are chosen."*

At first I was confused and thought perhaps I was dreaming. However, I was fully awake. I knew it was not a dream. Then suddenly a presence filled the room that was so overpowering. I began sobbing. I could not see anyone, but I could feel a strong presence. Next I began shaking very badly. Being concerned for my health sake, I began praying for the shaking to stop. Within minutes it stopped and I was left in awe as well as quite shaken by the experience. I had never before experienced such an event in my lifetime. I have been blessed to know many "special inspirational moments" in my life, but this experience was totally different. **I knew something wonderful** was going to happen. I shared this thought with a friend. **I just knew we were going to experience miracles.** I lived each day **in anticipation** of them.

We held our annual Fall garage sale, with proceeds going for the purchase of gifts for the children. As we were setting up, an electricity filled the air. I could feel it around me. I mentioned it to a friend who also felt it. Little did we know, God was going to heal some broken relationships during the sale. My friend and I were blessed to witness this wonderful event. We were so thankful and excited!

November had arrived and color filled trees were nearly barren. The winds were crisp and dried up leaves would blow from place to place. I received a call from a supporting group of church folks that our ministry would be remembered at their annual choir festival. This not only would bring our ministry to the attention of the community, but would help us reach out to more ill and needy youngsters through giving. I was delighted to receive the call, and always considered these calls a miracle.

Around this time, we were receiving urgent requests for new clothing, just like the year earlier. This year was a bit different as new hoodies topped the list of clothing needs. We were told many needy children did not have a warm winter jacket. I knew I could not afford to purchase a large quantity of hoodies, as they were very expensive. I did, however, agree to another "Only One" Clothing Drive. This meant flyers, ads, inquiries to businesses for drop-off locations – the rule of the day.

The Workshop was abuzz with activity. We added hoodies to our community list and did receive a few. The majority of clothing items received came in the form of hats, scarves, mittens and socks, also desperately needed. Knitted items as well as store items began **pouring in!** We passed the first goal of one thousand, then two thousand items, then three thousand beautiful warm pieces of clothing rested before our eyes. At each thousand level, I would ring a bell with joy and a thankfulness for God's wonderful storehouse of supply. **His blessings were flowing like a river.** Once again, a Divine Being heard a lady's prayer for His "little ones" and answered with a miracle as she prayed for warm hoodies.

You have read in a number of previous chapters about unexpected miraculous phone calls. Well, here came another phone call I shall never forget. It was from the family of our "dedicated elf" who had passed away. The voice on the other end of the phone asked me what the greatest need was at the moment.

I replied, "New hoodies."

I heard the question, "How many can you use?"

Knowing how expensive they were, I said we could use a few.

There was a pause; then I heard, "Could you use **six hundred new hoodies** with logos on them?"

I was speechless for a few moments and began crying. Could we use them? What a marvelous answer to prayer and what a miracle! My faith and trust in a loving God soared. My spirit seemed to be lifted high upon an angel's wing toward the Heavens, as a thankful lady fell to her knees.

On the evening of December 17th, the call was received stating the hoodies, sent from Austin, Texas, had arrived in a nearby city. They would be delivered that evening. Soon after, cartons upon cartons, huge in size, began filling the Workshop area of my home. It was a sight beyond belief! Each lovely warm hoodie with price tag attached, were **donated at no cost** to Santa's Workshop. We were now closing in on 4,000 pieces of new warm clothing. One more time, I would ring a bell in honor of a loving God. How blessed could one be! This giving touched the hearts of all participating this particular year.

Every miracle is special and unique. Yet, this miracle would touch an entire community, hundreds of children, Mrs. Claus and her "family of elves." Hundreds of little bodies were warmed from winter's chill. I know that giving couple have been blessed in life, as have I. I will be forever grateful for their generosity and caring.

My thoughts were drawn back to that early October morning and the prophetic words that resided within my being. There was a reason for that happening. There would be **more special moments** to follow.

That same evening as hundreds of hoodies were removed from their cartons, the sizing process began. These wonderful hoodies ranged in size from small to extra large. In order to fill requests efficiently, piles and piles of certain sized hoodies rose from table tops. As requests were filled, they were placed in Christmas tissue; then lovingly arranged in nicely proportioned boxes. What a sight to see!

As a busy evening progressed, the door bell rang. A Pastor friend had stopped by with a couple games for the children. When she saw piles and piles of hoodies, she was amazed and inquired as to how such an amount of hoodies had arrived at the Workshop. She then realized we needed help in processing, as only one other friend was helping size. She removed her coat and began a long evening of work that lasted into the morning hour.

Then a moment I shall never forget—this Pastor looked at my friend and me and said, "By the way, there are angels all around your house. I mean they are everywhere!" Needless to say, we stood there stunned. I had difficulty believing that statement, but then she added, "I don't make lightly of such matters." She could see the disbelief on my face and wished to assure me what she had related was true. She then told us as she turned onto my street she felt a large angelic presence in the area. When she entered my driveway angelic presence was felt all around my home. I will forever remember that stunning miraculous moment! I feel certain God sent angels to protect my earthly home, since so much activity was apparent.

Later on this same deeply spiritual lady would tell me that originally she had not planned on coming to the Workshop that evening. However, as she was leaving her church that evening, she saw two games in a collection box for Santa's Workshop. She then decided to drop them off, never imagining for a moment she should encounter a host of angels that special night.

The Lord decided to top that precious event with another one at our Dedication Service. This is a special service held at the Workshop in which all items are dedicated to the glory of God, for it is His blessing that rests upon this ministry. My Pastor friend was about to read from scripture. As she rose from her chair with Bible in hand, she turned to everyone and said, "We are standing on Holy Ground and there are angels in this room. They are all around us." In the silence that followed, folks attending that service were stunned and left in awe. Later I would ask her how that statement came about, since she was only to read a scripture. She said, "The Holy Spirit told me to tell you angels were present." Cold chills would ripple up and down my spine.

The next day, as I was vacuuming the carpet in the area where the service had been held, I noticed something lying on the floor. I walked over to the spot and beheld a soft billowy feather lying on the carpet right before my eyes. Was it an affirmation of angelic presence? I will leave you, the reader, to decide. For me, it was one more miraculous moment of an incredible journey. In my heart of hearts, I believe every word that was spoken was meant to be.

A taping was done during the service. When played back, **only loud static** could be heard. Might there have been a tremendous amount of electricity in the room that voided out the taping?

My heart bursting with excitement, processing moved forward. Calls from various churches enlightened all of us, as "new elves" joined in. Again, to see people of all different faiths and from all walks of life come together to help us fill thousands of requests, is a memory forever vivid in my mind.

I would like to share with you a heartwarming story of a grandmother and her grandson. He was ten years old at the time. His grandmother felt it would be nice for him to see what the Workshop looked like at holiday time. She hoped he would be able to understand why we were bringing joy to so many ill and needy children, and what really mattered beyond the gift.

They visited for a short time. As they were leaving the yard the little boy looked at his grandmother and said, "Meema, did you ever count how many times your life was changed in fifteen minutes? Mine was changed going into Mrs. Kinney's house tonight and meeting her. I'll never be the same."

When I was advised of this conversation, my heart and soul was deeply touched. It is my prayer and hope this young lad's life will never be the same. I hope what he experienced that evening will forever stay alive within him. I pray he will pass on to others the love and compassion he witnessed that special moment in time.

To inspire another human being is to light a candle within their soul. Our troubled world needs many, many "lit" candles.

The year 2009 was coming to a close. Rooms were stacked high with cartons of new clothing, hundreds of games, many stuffed animals and toys. We would load our "sleighs" to the count of over 4,000 new items of winter clothing and 1,682 additional "gifts of love." This came to a total of 5,682 donations; the greatest number of gifts Santa's Workshop had ever known. All gifts were given in memory of a faithful "elf" – "Elf T" who I'm sure was smiling down from a Heavenly realm.

Postscript to this chapter ~

Following the completion of all deliveries, it was time to focus on family, friends and thankfulness for a wonderful miraculous year. A dear friend and "elf" of Santa's Workshop was visiting a religious store in our area. As she walked in, there before her, was a sign that read **ANGELS CROSSING.** She said **she knew immediately** that sign was meant for the home in which Charles and I had answered the Lord's call for this ministry.

Today, all who visit are greeted by beautiful angel statues, standing tall among the flower gardens, along with a delightful sign reading ANGELS CROSSING. In certain gardens little cherubs dwell, **as a reminder of God's love** for His "little ones" here on earth. The sign reminds me that angels crossed our path and we crossed theirs this year of 2009. There is a smaller angel sign which reads "Angels are forever welcome here." Garden lights shine upon them each evening creating a warm, loving glow that says farewell to another blessed day of life. That glow will always fill my soul until the angels say "Amen."

Chapter 22

Doers of the Word

Be ye doers of the Word, not hearers only,
*deceiving your own selves. **James 1:22***

The cool, crisp breezes of Fall 2010 had arrived. I would make the decision to undertake yet another "Only One" Clothing Drive. The country's economy was taking severe blows from all directions and many people were losing their jobs. Family after family were hurting financially. The need for warm clothing would be our top priority.

Once again, I would take this urgent need to the community. Soon knitting needles were at work in the hands of many dedicated folks. Again, colors of the rainbow along with deep russet, orange, red and golden yellow would make up the spectrum of colors. It is such a joy to gaze upon the lovely "works of creation" which folks of all ages contributed. What a blessing to view items created by seniors in their eighties and nineties. How proud I am of everyone who shares their talent with others! They are "doers of the Word." They fill their hours with a hobby they enjoy. Then they bless others with their finished creations. They realize that **hearing of need and doing nothing means nothing. Hearing of need and doing whatever one can, means everything.**

Rooms at the Workshop were encumbered with toys, games, stuffed animals and activity sets from earlier months' purchases. We would receive the support of many folks in the community again this year, which always proved to be the greatest of blessing for all involved.

I would have the joy of visiting my family in West Virginia this Fall, just as I had done a year earlier. This always meant shopping for the children. Remember the saying–shop till you drop? That saying would prove true for my sister and me. We would visit every store in her area that she could think of, which carried toys and games. We would leave the stores with carts overflowing with sale items. What wonderful memories of the two of us laughing and joking with each other as our arms were weighed down with packages of all kinds and sizes.

This particular time we found wonderful Tonka puzzle books. They were a thick, weighty book and when you had over a dozen of them to carry through a mall, you faced a challenge. Our fingers would turn numb, but we would laugh all the harder until tears wet our cheeks. What "beautiful moments" in time, making glad the heart of a child, while being "doers of the Word."

This Fall, I would return to Santa's Workshop at Angels Crossing with a carload of "love gifts" to brighten the hearts and lives of many ill and needy children. The Lord had filled my sister's heart and mine with a **deep love** for His "little ones" and a **joy within us** for special moments shared together. When families are separated by hundreds of miles many special moments in life are missed. What fun and joy when these moments do occur and we can make each moment count for something special.

The holidays were now upon us. Wrapping of the activity sets became the order of the day. Fifteen hundred items would need to be arranged into three hundred sets; then wrapped in brightly colored children's wrapping paper. A very sweet little neighbor girl loved to visit the Workshop and arrange the sets for wrapping. Her little face glowed like stars. She would say "I'm so excited!"

Years earlier, when she was very small, her mother stopped by one day and showed her daughter hundreds of gifts already processed for delivery. I remember watching this lovely lady kneel down by the gifts; then explained to her daughter where these gifts were going and why. It was a touching moment indeed. Over the course of the next few years this caring family would surprise Mrs. Claus with delightful gifts. Remember the surprise gift of basketballs? Now, two little girls would ring the doorbell smiling from ear to ear, each holding something special for a less fortunate child. These times would be so special, creating wonderful memories for them and for me, a "treasure chest" of memories to open later in life.

The weeks of activity passed swiftly. It was time for our dedication service, a time we would thank God for all blessings received through Him. Blessings would be sought for all the child recipients, their families, and all our "elves" throughout the community. It is always a most inspirational time. A time when my heart overflows with gratitude for the time, talents, and gifts of everyone who once again chose to make a difference in another human life. On this particular Saturday afternoon, ministers, friends and "elves" began arriving. Just minutes before the service was to begin, the doorbell rang. There stood this little neighbor girl and her family laden with holiday bags of gifts for children. Games, toys, stuffed animals and dollies all peeking out from their respective packages. This little girl had turned **seven years old**. Instead of her friends giving her gifts for her birthday, she asked them to bring a gift for a less fortunate child instead.

With her little face beaming with joy, she said to me, "I want to do this for the children." All gifts were presented to me for Santa's Workshop for Hospitalized Children. I can tell you there was barely a dry eye in the room full of people, as well as mine. This child made such an impression on the adults gathered that one of the ministers spoke to her congregation the next day, telling them of this loving little girl. Many hearts were touched that afternoon. Years earlier, this little girl learned at her mother's knee what giving and caring was all about and she remembered. There is a saying, "a child shall lead them." In this case, that is exactly what happened. A child led all of us to an ever deeper commitment to make a difference in the life of another. **To find a need and fill it; to find a hurt and heal it.**

Delivery time had arrived and with it came the cold elements of winter. Loaded sleighs would be accompanied by heavy wet snow and icy conditions under foot. Spirits were high despite the harsh elements. In the meantime, I had caught a cold that would cancel my visits to the bedside of the hospitalized children. This saddened me a great deal and I remember speaking to the Lord about it. I would miss the opportunity to see a child's face light up with a glow of happiness upon receiving a surprise gift. However, I needed to focus on the delivery of gifts.

Upon arriving at the hospital, the weather was a snowy, rainy mix. It was recommended I stay inside the medical building where we were unloading, due to my cold. I sat on a bench in the main corridor watching all the cartons of lovely gifts pass by me, disappearing down the hallway to the storage area. As I'm sitting there watching the activity, to the right of me, down the hallway, came a little boy with his mother. They were the only folks I had seen outside of our helpers. As this little boy drew near, he stopped by the bench, climbed up beside me, his mother sitting at his side. As he watched more and more toys and stuffed animals pass by, he turned to his mother and asked, "Is somebody having a party?"

His mother's reply was, "I don't know, honey."

Then a light bulb went off in my head. I had shared my sadness with the Lord about not being able to visit the children personally, but here beside me was this darling little boy full of wonder. I had been sent a little child to make happy that day. I jumped up as the next group of cartons were brought in from the "sleigh." I spoke to the young lad carrying the carton and asked to see the inside. There lay the sweetest puppy with a card game attached to its little body. I removed him from the carton, approached the little boy and wished him a Merry Christmas as I presented him with the puppy. The look on that little face was worth a thousand words. He climbed off the bench, wrapped his little arms around my legs, as I stood in the hallway, and thanked me for the puppy. His Mom sat there beaming and thanked me for making his day a special one.

Had a Divine Being heard those few concerned words I had spoken earlier? Had He seen the sadness in Mrs. Claus? I not only believe He heard, but answered that sadness with a moment of joy between a little boy and a lady with a heart full of love. He sent me a child to share with and I will always cherish that special moment.

As we were leaving that day, the Child Life Specialist told me about a little girl who had been very listless since her arrival there a few days earlier. No child is happy to be in strange surroundings, feeling ill, especially at holiday time. She asked me if it would be all right if she took a "special" large teddy bear to her that afternoon even though it was a couple of days before Santa's bedside visit. I told her, "Of course, take her whatever you feel might gladden her heart."

A bit later I would hear the result of that early visit. As the lovely Christmas bear was presented to the child, she lay there very quiet just looking at the bear in the arms of the specialist. She assured the child the teddy bear was truly for her. Then within the wink of a moment, this child jumped up on the bed, grasped the teddy bear and hugged it tightly. After being tucked back in bed with teddy at her side, this little girl spoke to the bear, "We will watch pictures." (It is believed she meant TV). As the Child Life Specialist began walking away, a little voice called out to her, **"Merry Kissmas!"** One more sad and frightened ill child **found comfort in a "new friend"** given by a stranger to a stranger's child–someone who believes in the words "be a doer."

As the year of 2010 came to a close, Santa's sleighs would carry 3,300 gifts through the snow to the ill and needy. Of that figure, 2,100 new warm items of clothing were distributed.

Yes, the bell would ring three times—once for the first thousand pieces of warm clothing, then once more for the second thousand. **Then one more time to thank and give praise to a loving Heavenly Father who loves His little children.** Yellow, red, black or white, they are all precious in His sight.

Chapter 23

The Spirit and the Glow of Hope

Now hope does not disappoint, because the love of God has been poured out in our hearts by the Holy Spirit who was given to us. **Romans 5:5**

Hope, a tiny word of only four letters, holds a huge meaning behind it. Over the years, Santa's Workshop has stood out as a "beacon" for many. This ministry has held high its candles of **love, compassion, faith, belief** and **trust** throughout the community. Yet, there has been one more candle that has glowed through the darkness; **the candle of hope**. This candle is inspired within each of us, and guided by a Divine Spirit.

Hope for recovery from illness, hope for a miracle, hope for a new beginning, hope for an end to adversity, hope for today's tribulations, and hope for a better and kinder tomorrow all cry out from the human spirit. These cries of the soul, when interwoven with a Divine Spirit, bring us hope.

Can a stuffed animal to cuddle offer hope as well as comfort? Can a dolly to hold and tuck into bed stir hope within a troubled heart? Can a warm hat, hoodie, and mittens give a needy child hope?

This Fall of 2011, Santa's Workshop at Angels Crossing would, once again, light its candle of hope for the ill and needy. Many "little ones" would be inspired by the candle of hope that would accompany their Santa gift. **We do not always need to see in order to feel!**

When a child has been severely abused, that child needs to feel hope. When a child receives a frightening diagnosis, hope is needed. A displaced child feels a void in life–a void that needs to be replenished with hope. As mentioned earlier, **hope is a cry of the soul**. We all need hope!

This particular Fall would bring many joys. One more clothing drive would top our agenda. One "elf" who loves to knit every available hour she can find would top out at a little over three thousand knitted items since she began knitting for our ministry. One human being with three thousand beautiful "items of hope." What a difference she has made in the lives of ill and needy children and their families. It proves, once again, what even one person is capable of doing, if the heart and mind is willing.

In October I would again visit my family down south. My sister and I would shop for the children while enjoying each other's company. While making our rounds from store to store, we discovered some adorable talking bears. They were absolutely precious as they spoke five different sayings. I was able to purchase them at half price. I was very excited about this opportunity, as they were very expensive bears. Normally I would not have been able to afford them, but right at the time I was there they were on a special promotion. I knew they would bring so much joy and hope to a hurting child. Another car load of gifts returned to Angels Crossing and we were on our way to another exciting season.

As the weeks passed I realized we were desperately in need of dolls. I visited store after store and could not afford any doll purchases. Pricing was out of sight for our small budget. Once again, I found myself standing in a doll aisle in a store, praying for an answer to this need.

A couple days later as I was walking through a room in my home, words rose up within me. These words were the name of a website on the internet. At the time, I was a "rookie" with computers and did not know many computer functions. After hearing the words twice I turned my new

189

computer on, hoping and praying that I could find my way to this particular site. I had never been on it before. I slowly found my way onto the website. There I found a listing of garage sales and individual items that were for sale. After scrolling through a number of garage sales, standing out before my eyes was a listing which read: "huge doll sale, new dolls in boxes." I found the address, jumped in the car and I was off to the listed location.

When I arrived I walked into a garage that had been turned into a doll paradise. There were dolls wherever I looked. My heart leapt within me. I remember telling God how badly I needed some of these dolls for His "little ones." As the lady waited on a few customers I just browsed and prayed. All of a sudden the lady approached me saying, "There are a lot of dolls here. If you are interested in any of them, just ask me the price. I have too many to tag. I have at least a thousand dolls."

Thoughts began whirling around in my head. Then the strangest thing happened. It was opening morning of the sale; yet, it became very quiet. No one else stopped by for some time. During this lapse the lady approached me again and said, "When my sale is over, I'm going to be looking for some place to donate a number of these dolls." I could not believe what I was hearing. I immediately introduced myself and our ministry, telling the lady about the children we had served over the years. I explained the need I had for dolls. She inquired if I had any paperwork and pictures she could review. I excitedly told her I did. Could I return with those requested items, I was asked. After purchasing several dolls at a fraction of the original cost, I assured her I would return.

The next morning I returned at the opening hour with all requested items in hand. After reviewing the papers and pictures, the lady smiled, gave me a hug and said, "You know, honey, God answers prayer. You will have a number of dolls for the children at Christmas. I will donate them to your project. The light that crosses your face when you speak of the children spoke to my heart."

This wonderful caring lady was true to her word. Several weeks later, as the holiday neared, I received her call. A **car load of unopened packages of new dollies** were waiting for Santa's sleigh. Again, I felt I was soaring heavenward on angel wings. This lady was definitely an earthly angel for the children and me. Many little girls received a new dolly from Santa's pack as he visited ward to ward. A few others in different circumstances also received a new dolly.

What joy and hope these children received on our Savior's birthday. I believe to this day a Divine Spirit touched this lady's spirit and together hope was born. Hope for a better tomorrow for each child. Also this lady's spirit was inspired by the love within my spirit for these less fortunate "little ones" who are part of His Kingdom.

One more answer to sincere prayer being offered up in a store aisle, creating one more wonderful miracle from a miracle working God. A God whose Divine Spirit leads us forth on His pathway of hope.

Then another "special moment" would be mine to savor. The sweet little girl mentioned in the former chapter of this book, would grace Angels Crossing with her love and compassion for others a second time. She had now turned eight years old. Once again she advised her little friends of her wish to share her birthday gifts with less fortunate children. She arrived laden down with bags of toys, games and stuffed animals. Again her little face glowed with joy; her beautiful eyes sparkling with delight. I could feel my tear ducts filling with moisture as I hugged this little "earthly angel." Why do I call her a little "earthly angel?"

A while later I decided to rearrange her wonderful gifts for a picture. As I removed one remaining gift from the floor to place with the others, there lay a small baby soft white feather. It lay in the exact spot where the remaining gift had rested. I have kept the feather as a reminder that angels can appear in all sizes. Often times they leave a reminder behind that we may have entertained an angel unaware.

I would like to add, that yes, I checked all items to see if anything contained feathers. Not one item did. This truly was a touching moment–a moment to add to my "treasure chest" of memories.

As our time of the dedication of gifts approached, there was an excitement in the air. We would be blessed to have two harpists providing the music for the service. A Pastor friend and her granddaughter would touch the hearts of all attending. As we lifted our praises toward Heaven, the melodious sound of the harps truly placed us on Holy Ground. We did not need to wonder if angels were present, we knew they were singing God's praises with us because they abide at Angels Crossing. Every little while they drop a feather letting me know they have crossed my pathway one more time. One more time I have been allowed to serve a Divine Being and His children.

Just a few days later we would experience a "special moment" in the Pediatric Ward of the hospital where we had just delivered 2,237 Santa gifts. According to the nurse that day, a young girl, who had been admitted a few days earlier was unresponsive to their attempts to befriend her. The "elves" and I were visiting the Ward accompanied by several large special stuffed animals. The nurse said to me, "May I take her one of these? Maybe that would help. We just can't get her to respond to us."

She took one of the large bears into her as we waited in the hallway. A few minutes later this nurse came out of the room very excited, a huge smile crossing her face. With such relief in her voice, she said, "She responded to the bear. Thank you, thank you. You made a difference." A quiver passed through her voice and her eyes appeared moist.

All the "elves" in that hallway began crying. One of my "elves" came over and took my hand. She looked at me and said, "Did you hear that?" I nodded my head as I, too, was crying. We had just experienced a wonderful moment where hope was born anew and a human life touched.

What made that serene moment even more special, a little boy and girl had traveled three thousand miles cross country with their mother to visit relatives and Santa's Workshop. They witnessed this special moment in the hallway. They had passed this particular bear to the nurse along with another stuffed animal that was delivered to a little boy in the next room. That little boy, we were told was going to be there for some time. He, too, had a new friend to fill his heart with hope. I have often wondered what the unresponsive little girl found in that large teddy bear that she did not find in human contact. Could it have been that she felt she had **something tangible** to hold onto; something that belonged only to her? Only our Lord knows what lay within her heart. What matters is that a way was found to help bring her out of her withdrawal. A stranger's love had touched her and brought her hope.

Teddy bears and angel bears, I truly believe, have a special purpose here on earth. I have never seen a time when they failed to make a difference. They always brighten a life, even when a child is on his or her way to Heaven.

I will always remember those haunting words of a dying child rocking her angel bear in her arms saying, "You're all mine, you're all mine."

This year of 2011, loaded sleighs arrived at all locations safely and on time carrying 3,250 "gifts of hope" to the less fortunate. New warm clothing totaled 2,173 items. The remainder of 1,077 items would consist of toys, stuffed animals, book sets and games. All totaled since 1989, the unbelievable rounded sum of 54,000 children have known a "moment of joy" through gifts of love, compassion, and hope. Each gift has carried with it a Divine Spirit pouring out Jesus' love, and blessing each child recipient with hope. Hope for a better tomorrow; hope for a kinder and more compassionate world.

Chapter 24

The Vine and the Branch

*"I am the Vine, ye are the branches: He that abideth in me, and I in Him, the same bringeth forth **much fruit**; for without me, ye can do nothing. If ye abide in me, and my words abide in you, ye shall ask what ye will, and it shall be done unto you. **Herein is my Father glorified, that ye bear much fruit**; so shall ye be my disciples." **John 15:5, 7, 8***

Everyone on earth has a story to share. Not everyone shares their story. For the longest time I was one of those persons who realized there was a story to be told. Yet, I could not reach the point of writing the story on paper. The main reason—I felt inadequate to tell the **Lord's story** through Charles' and my story. That always was and is the priority wish of my heart, **to tell His story**. How does one give an awesome Divine Being the glory, laud, and honor due Him? I have searched for that answer for some time. Now the answer has been made clear for me. It is found in his Holy Word.

I am writing this last chapter on a beautiful sunny summer afternoon in the year 2012. As I gaze out the window at the woods, a brisk warm breeze caresses the leaves. It reminds me of the scripture that says the wind blows and we hear the sound. Yet, we do not know when it is coming nor where it shall go. Likewise, as I close this chapter, I have no idea where the Lord's Spirit will take these words nor when. However, I do know His Spirit covers the words on the pages. **He will decide** whom to inspire and in what way.

You may wonder who or what was behind the success of this ministry. From its very beginning, Jesus Christ has been our Vine, the central core of everything. We have been His branches, grafted to Him. Should you wonder what I'm referring to, may I explain?

The Vine and the branch is a living union. It is a living, personal relationship through the Holy Spirit with the person of Jesus as the core of the union. We are dependent upon Him to provide and meet each need in life. We receive into our life, His life, that we may live abundantly and carry His life to others. His life flows in and through us making it a continuous union.

Charles and I have always felt humbled and grateful for the calling we received. Without that calling and without seeking His will for our lives, this book would have never taken place. There could not have been a ministry to share with others. I write this inspirational story with such thankfulness to a God of provision.

I write it from the heart of a child who has experienced an incredible journey. I write it from a couple whose lives were taken to heights never dreamed possible. I also write it from a hurting child's heart; a child who knows fear and uncertainty. But foremost, I write this story to give praise to an awesome, majestic Divine Being who is the author of all things. I could never speak enough words or write enough pages of the love and adoration I feel for this Divine Being.

I have often envisioned a grape clinging to the vine. Upon receiving sunlight and water, it grows strong and to its fullness. With nurturing it becomes a delectable fruit. A fruit that brings delight to one's taste buds. A fruit that has a purpose in life.

The scripture for this closing chapter speaks of the fruits we are to bear in His name, when attached to Him. The fruits we are to share with one another. As a branch of the Vine, we are fed through the Vine, the fruits we are to share with each other. When we bear fruit and touch a life for Him, **WE GLORIFY HIM** then and there. Jesus said,

"Herein is my Father glorified, **that ye bear much fruit**. Therein I found the answer to my question.

Our ministry has been filled with many fruits of the Vine. Fruits such as love, compassion, hope, faith, trust, generosity, answered prayer and miracles. **Through the working of His Spirit**, these fruits have touched thousands of lives.

I ask you this, dear friend–would you like to taste of these fruits? Would you be interested in becoming a branch of the Vine? He is waiting for you, just as He was waiting for us. We needed encouragement, so the Lord sent us His messengers. Now he sends me to be His messenger for you and to share His good news in a darkened world. He holds out to us His candle, but it is we who must light that candle and be willing to carry it where ever we go. All it takes is **one more lit candle to lessen the darkness. You and I can be that light!**

It is my soulful prayer that as our journey together comes to an end, it will be a **new beginning** for you. A brand new journey can be yours, if you are willing to step out in faith, and onto a new pathway of service to others. What makes it so exciting is you do not have to walk it alone. You have a Vine to cling to, a blessed companion to walk with you all the way. Not for an hour, not for a day, not for a year, but **alway!**

How warm and wonderful you will feel when you are the reason for a broad smile to cover a saddened face. To hear the words, "You have made me happy" or the touching words, "God Bless you for caring." How touched you will be when tears wash the face of a hurting soul and you hear the words, "You are an angel." I know because I have heard those inspiring words many times and I have been blessed. I have become ever more humble, for I have realized that without the blessing and work of the Lord's Spirit within me, those words would never be mine to savor.

In Isaiah 45:6 we read these words: *That they may know from the rising of the sun to its setting that there is none besides me. I am the Lord and there is none else.*

As I write this, Fall is only weeks away. Already two rooms are filling with stuffed animals, toys and games. Cartons of coloring books, fun pads and crayons are stored away. Readers are neatly lined on shelving awaiting the reader. Many rag dollies and adorable stuffed animals fill large bags to capacity. This year I visited family early and found dollies I have been searching for the past three years. They are so cute and colorful. They wait to be held, hugged, and to tickle a little girl's heart. The first of many God winks?

Over five hundred pieces of knitted and store purchased clothing items have been received. Knitting needles are already busy. I just learned an "elf" has over one hundred knitted baby hats ready for delivery to Santa's Workshop. I am already anticipating a wonderful new season of giving. Mrs. Claus cannot wait to see the miracles God has in store for us this year. Each one will be different and unique and will lift our spirits.

I am well along on my journey now. Time is passing swiftly. Soon there will be another "calling" for another human being to continue what has begun. The candle must remain lit. I am so pleased that two former "elves" of Santa's Workshop now have ministries of their own. Each year at holiday time they take hundreds of gifts to needy children both locally and in another area of the state of New York. I am so proud of these "elves" that are making a difference in the lives of many less fortunate children. Perhaps you would help me keep the flame burning?

Yes, we began with **two little toy trucks** for two little brothers in strange surroundings on Christmas Day. Twenty three years later, 54,000 "Santa" gifts of love and hope have brought comfort and a "moment of joy" to His "little ones." Not only locally, but thousands of miles away in other states and across the water.

Paths have crossed, love has reached out and lives have been transformed. There have been stories of answered prayer, miracles, angels and feathers. Stories of community coming together for a common purpose. Stories of a Christmas where there was going to be none. Stories of "forgotten" children who know little of a fulfilled life, and stories of the dying who found comfort in an angel teddy bear.

I pray your heart has been touched. I pray you found inspiration on this journey with Charles and me.

Now, may all glory, laud and honor rise on the wings of angels to an awesome and majestic God who made it all possible. A God who in His infinite love reached down to earth and granted a man and a woman an incredible journey.

Amen.